BOUNCING BACK

REFLECTIONS ON RESILIENT WOMEN IN THE PENTATEUCH

Dr. D. Robert Kennedy, Ed. D; Ph.D
With a Foreword by Dr. S. June Kennedy, Ed.D

© 2019 by D. Robert Kennedy

Published by Legacy Seminars LLC
    11503 Belvidere Road
    Bowie MD 20721
    Legacyseminars41@gmail.com

Printed in the United States of America

All rights reserved. No part of this publication may be reproduced, stored in a retrieval system, or transmitted in any form means – for example, electronic, photocopy, recording - without the prior written permission of the publisher. The only exception is brief quotations in printed reviews.

ISBN: 978-1-7321890-6-5

Scripture quotations are taken from:

Scripture taken from the New King James Version®. Copyright © 1982 by Thomas Nelson. Used by permission. All rights reserved.

All Scripture quotations, unless otherwise indicated, are taken from the Holy Bible, New International Version®, NIV®. Copyright ©1973, 1978, 1984, 2011 by Biblica, Inc.™ Used by permission of Zondervan. All rights reserved worldwide

DEDICATED

To the women of the Emmanuel Worship Center, who have demonstrated what it means to be faithful in the prayer ministry, and service ministries, especially at this time of replanting our church. You have sacrificed much, and this is why you are so highly appreciated. It is my prayer that your salvation will be made secure and that all of the divine blessings may attend you in your struggles of life. As you live in our topsy-turvy world, you will face times when you fall, but be assured that the Lord who has lifted the women who have fallen, will lift you.

TABLE OF CONTENTS

Foreword 1

A Plan Of Restoration And Transformation For Women 7

A First Great Blessing For Women 11

The Fall And The Rise Of Mother Eve 17

The Daughters Of Men 23

Women In The Ark 29

A Woman Under Pressure 35

Remember Lot's Wife 41

Lot's Daughters 47

Dealing With Delay 53

Sarah's Advice 59

A Favor For The Unfavored 65

Resentment Is Not The Solution 71

Returning To An Oppressive Situation 77

The God Who Sees 83

Sarah And The Sacrifice Of Isaac 89

The Death Of Sarah 93

The Influence Of A Matriarch 99

The Right Woman For A Wife 105

She Will Be Good For You 111

Helping Out God 117

Double Crossing A Sister 123

Not So Beautiful, But Blessed 129

Sitting On An Idol 135

The Death Of A Rival Sister 141

The Tragedy Of Rape 147

The Death Of A Caregiver 153

Marrying For The Right Reason 159

Living In A Culture Of Oppression 165

She Said He Did It 171

When A Mixed Marriage Becomes A Blessing 177

The Resisters 183

The Protective Mother 189

A Caring Sister 195

The Adoptive Mother 201

Helpers Become Silent Resisters 207

Beyond Intuition 213

Dealing With Taboos 219

Artistic Women 225

Social Activists 231

Bouncing Back 237

Conclusion 243

FOREWORD

Reflecting on the joys and sorrows, the blessings and curses, the rise and the fall, the downfall and uprising of women in the Bible, especially of those in the early patriarchal history, is profoundly fascinating. I am a lover of history and have read several books written about such women, by women, but it is quite impressive when one can see and read a masculine author up close and see how his views on such women find their place into the perspectives he puts in public view. Working with my husband as he wrote his weekly opinion editorials called "From the Pastor's Heart," for the Local Talk Newspaper in Newark/Orange, New Jersey, has offered me the privilege of a first editor's read about the women. However, writing this Foreword has helped me to identify with some of the emotions that impacted my husband, that I did not note as he wrote.

When my husband began to collect the pieces for the book, I suggested to him a few titles. He settled on the one I framed, *Bouncing Back: A Legacy of Blessings for Women,* which truly reflects what I think is most central to the lives of most of the women in the volume. The collection focuses on the lives of the women from Genesis through Deuteronomy. The book reminds me that, in spite of the difficulties many women faced and the deficits in their own lives, God has always been ready to work powerfully through these complexities, to help them on the path of redemption.

The Apostle Paul writes, "For the grace of God that brings salvation has appeared to **all men**," (Titus 2:11 NKJV). If he were writing in more contemporary times, he would have explicitly used language to include women as well. It is clear that the grace of which he speaks has been given to women, like men, through all the generations of humanity. Just as it is said, "Noah found grace in the eyes of the Lord" (Genesis 6:8), it can be said that Noah's wife and daughters in law, the women in the ark, also found grace in the eyes of the Lord.

When one thinks of Eve, the mother of all living, as profiled in the Bible, one is tempted to think of her name as being synonymous with the fall of humanity and thus the woes that we now encounter. But how does one think of the powerful legacy of blessing she left on the world? This question is one of the many issues that Bouncing Back seeks to answer. We have also heard about Sarah and her actions. Was she always the lying, submissive, resentful mother who she is often portrayed to be? This book gives clear answer. But if you feel like Sarah and any such character, God's forgiveness is for the asking. And the seeker has this assurance of forgiveness from Micah 7:17 NIV, "Who is a God like you, who pardons sin and forgives the transgression of the remnant of his inheritance? You do not stay angry forever but delight to show mercy." Yes, he shows mercy to every woman who comes boldly to the throne of grace to find pardon and peace. Each must heed this admonition, "If any of you lacks wisdom, you should ask God, who gives generously to all without finding fault, and it will be given to you. [6] But when you ask, you must believe and not doubt because the one who doubts is like a wave of the sea, blown and tossed by the wind. (James 1: 5-6 NIV).

If you knew the author of this book, *Bouncing Back,* as I do, you would understand that his purpose for writing is not just to put forth another manuscript. Instead, he is seeking to use biblical models, ranging from the courageous to the weak, the prominent to the obscure, the understood to the misunderstood, the accused to the praised, to focus on the vast possibilities in the lives of women. He also shows how God uses women from every walk of life to accomplish his purposes, just as he uses men. This desire to focus on women is not only from a mere academic understanding of research but instead, from deep insights grounded in his ability to perceive what might propel a woman to action. I dare say that his insights have legitimacy, based on a deep sense of empathy. Over the years, I have heard, and I have watched the author's reactions when he sees women being trivialized, being oppressed, disenfranchised, or being disrespected. And he has been quick to call out the wrongs against women, and help in the search for amelioration.

The author grew up with five sisters and four brothers. Even though he was the middle child, the circumstances of his life made him the fiercest defender of even his sisters, who were older than himself, as well as the younger ones. He did what was necessary – physical fights, waiting on them for long hours to ensure their safety, even being very involved in ensuring that they received the dreams of their education. Even though his sisters are now adults, he is still their defender by giving them a voice when needed, clarifying misunderstandings, voicing the unspoken, and advocating for them when needed.

My conviction is that the attitude of selflessness and caring has never left this author. Whether as a pastor, administrator, or college professor, he has taken the stance of seeking for justice, of protecting the weak and vulnerable. I've seen him working arduously to restore women when they have fallen from grace and marginalized within the church community. Early in his ministry, the author refused to dedicate babies born to unwed mothers in the church office and under a tree in the churchyard as was done by so many pastors. He saw such punitive actions as unacceptable and demeaning, especially when the young men seem to be getting a "free ride." Very early in his ministry, he advocated for change and made the change within his pastoral circuit. In the early 1980s, when it was unpopular in churches to elect female elders and even ordain them, without deep thought of the consequences for himself, the author saw to the election of two women as elders. Within a short period of time, these two were ordained. The author said that the Spirit of God was subverting the strictures of traditions. He saw the women's dedication and commitment to the cause of God and did not see reasons to stand in the way of their opportunity in ministry.

Because of his initial disgust and distrust for the treatment of women, Dr. Kennedy, plunged himself into deep reflections on women, both from the Bible and secular history. The course Religion and Gender that he wrote and taught at Atlantic Union College are still remembered fondly by students. Dr. Kennedy argues that women, whether they are popular or unpopular, prominent or obscure, challenged or without challenges, may fall, but rise, and can bounce back from the most tragic of circumstances.

If you want to understand more about the hearts of the women in the Pentateuch and what they can teach us to do or not do, read *Bouncing Back: A Legacy Blessings for Women*. Each woman in this volume has a unique story and plays a unique role. To fully comprehend the impact each has made and can make on our lives, one must read the volume. See how Dr. Kennedy imagines the incomplete stories. Most of all, enjoy how loudly the voiceless can speak.

S. June E. Kennedy

A PLAN OF RESTORATION AND TRANSFORMATION FOR WOMEN

And I will put enmity
Between you and the woman,
And between your seed and her seed;
He shall bruise your head,
And you shall bruise His heel."

— Genesis 3:15 NKJV

A PLAN OF RESTORATION AND TRANSFORMATION FOR WOMEN

It is profoundly fascinating to see how God has taken women on the periphery and made them central in the plan of salvation. When they have fallen to the worst, God sees them in light of their circumstances and in light of eternity. In the midst of their failures and distresses, God is ever seeking to bring restoration and transformation to them. Such is the story of the majority of the women on whom we base the present reflections from Genesis through Deuteronomy or the five books of Moses known as the Pentateuch.

When, for example, one takes a look at the lives of women such as Leah, Tamar, Rebecca, and Asenath, one cannot say less than that "For the grace of God that brings salvation has appeared to all human beings." (Titus 2:11). Which is to say that the grace of God can reach women, at any time, in any place.

Women of grace are women who have experienced change, not sex change, but character change. Women of grace can appreciate their authentic femininity. They value the dignity that God has given to them, and they praise God for their lives in God.

It must also note that the women who have Bounced Back by grace were trailblazers. As imperfect as many of their lives have been, they have had a profound influence on succeeding generations. It must be painful to

God when his daughters cast themselves into a life of misery. It must hurt him when they fail to appreciate the joy and happiness for which he created them.

These reflections are intended to challenge any woman who would make her life one of misery instead of the life of joy that is available to everyone. Never should one allow himself/herself to be confused by beauty, personal indulgence, uncontrolled passion, cultural tradition, or anything that makes of one a negative character.

God has made you as a sister in God's image. Treasure the image. If you fall, get back up, ask God to cleanse you, and to give you his robe of righteousness. God bless you as you read on.

Reflecting on the discussion

1. What new insights that you have gained from the discussion?

2. What experience have you faced that could have turned into defeat, but by God's grace, has turned into a triumph?

3. Write a blessing that you desire for today, and for which you need to pray.

A FIRST GREAT BLESSING FOR WOMEN

¹⁸ And the Lord God said, "*It is* not good that man should be alone; I will make him a helper comparable to him." ²¹ And the Lord God caused a deep sleep to fall on Adam, and he slept, and He took one of his ribs and closed up the flesh in its place. ²² Then the rib which the Lord God had taken from man He made into a woman, and He brought her to the man.
²³ And Adam said:
"This *is* now bone of my bones
And flesh of my flesh;
She shall be called Woman,
Because she was taken out of Man."
²⁴ Therefore a man shall leave his father and mother and be joined to his wife, and they shall become one flesh.
²⁵ And they were both naked, the man and his wife, and were not ashamed.

Genesis 2:18, 21-25 NKJV

A FIRST GREAT BLESSING FOR WOMEN

Can you imagine living in a world where women and men are treated equally? Can you imagine a world in which there is no need for an EEOC (Equal Employment Opportunity Commission)? Where there is no need for Promundo? No need for CARE? No need for a White Ribbon? No need for a NOW Foundation? No need for organizations dedicated to closing the gender gap or protecting and improving the lives of women and girls? Just imagine no calls about sexual harassment, rape, and all the negatives that diminish the lives of women. Can you envision such a world?

Let me introduce you to such a world, as I have read it in the Bible. Yes, I accept by faith, that there was such a world. Before any curse was pronounced on the earth, there was such a world. That was the world in which God gave humanity a blessing. The first blessing was fixed in the creation of the first human family when God took a rib out of Adam's side and made Eve as a "*Help Meet*" for him (Genesis 2:18).

What is the significance of the word "helpmeet?" The Kings James Version translates the Hebrew phrase עזר כנגדו (*ezer kenegedo*) as "help meet for him." Other versions provide additional translations including; "a helper fit for him" (RSV), "a helper as his partner" (NRS), "a helper comparable to him" (NKJV), and "a helper as his counterpart" (YLT).

Some time ago, I heard a reflection on the helper in a powerful sermon by a woman, titled "Adam's Alter Ego." That is someone who was his other half, "one like himself," one who served as an "opposite self." Although I had studied the concept in my theological research, I was fascinated that a woman was preaching it.

In Genesis 1:27, we read that God - *Elohiym*, filled *Adam* (the Hebrew word for humanity) with his shadow, placed a representation of himself in the man. We also read in this verse that *Elohiym filled* them, male and female, meaning that he put within each his attributes- the male attributes in the man, and the feminine attributes in the woman. Some people often do not think of *Elohiym* as having male and female traits, but there are many passages in the Bible, reflecting this idea. I invite you to research them.

What is most significant is that at the creation of humanity, the world was one of perfect harmony. There was untainted love. There was respect between the genders. The holy couple understood their relationship roles. They were not arguing over who would train the vines or who would gather food for supper. There was no discrimination and resentment toward each other. There was no blaming and shaming of each other. We read of the pleasurable life in Genesis 2:26, 27, this way:

> For this reason, a man will leave his father and mother and be united to his wife, and they will become one flesh. And the man and his wife were both naked, and they were not ashamed. (Genesis 2:26, 27).

In effect, the couple in Eden trusted each other in such a way, that they were wholly vulnerable with each other. There was no struggle about who would submit to whom. It must have been wonderful when Eve lived as the first bride of Eden. She must have been:

1. Very happy (with her lover)
2. Living the good life (without sin)
3. Breathing the untainted air (abundant living)
4. Enjoying the restful days (Sabbath in Eden)
5. Clothe in light (Naked but not ashamed. Not dressed in fig leaves)
6. Enjoying the one-flesh intimacy (No competing person or persons in the relationship)
7. Felt freed in the presence of the divine (No hiding from God under a brush)
8. Relishing the tree of life

To me, it is not childish to let the imagination reflect on the harmony in Eden, because it is in the hearts of human beings to look back to Eden and wish for an Eden on earth again. Some have put it into Utopian dreams. Others follow the revealed word of God, where God says that he "will make all things new" (Revelation 21:5). If we share the latter vision, we can wait for a day to let Mother Eve tell us her story. She will be glad, I am sure, for Eden restored.

Reflecting on the discussion

1. What new insights that you have gained from the discussion?

2. Has there been any experience you faced that could have turned into defeat, but, by God's grace, has turned into a triumph?

3. Write a blessing that you desire for today, and for which you need to pray.

THE FALL AND THE RISE OF MOTHER EVE

¹⁵ And I will put enmity
Between you and the woman, And between your seed and her seed;
He shall bruise your head,
And you shall bruise His heel."

Genesis 3:15 NKJV

THE FALL AND THE RISE OF MOTHER EVE

At the beginning of the congressional year, as Nancy Pelosi became the Speaker of the United States Congress for a second time, I began to think of the resilience of women. Nancy Pelosi is the first woman to serve as Speaker of the Congress. She first served as Speaker, from 2007-2011 and again in 2019. She lost her speakership when her party lost, but she is back, roaring with very little opposition, even from her party. If there is a woman who profiles resiliency, it is Nancy Pelosi.

Of course, before Nancy Pelosi, there was Mother Eve. According to the Biblical story, she is the mother of all living beings. She, like her husband Adam, was created in the image of God. Together they were given responsibilities to care for the earth. One day while she was apart from Adam, she succumbed to the serpent's temptation. She "fell," and in turn, Adam disobeyed God and followed his wife, Eve. The story, as told in Genesis 3, is called "the fall" in Christian understanding. The Fall is used to explain the transition from the time of innocence to the time of sin and guilt in which the world finds itself today. The consequences of the Fall are multitudinous. Here is a list of ten:

1. The separation that took place between God and human beings
2. The degradation of relationships between Eve and Adam, and the future families of the earth

3. The blaming and shaming that began in Eden between Eve and Adam has become a historical reality among humanity
4. The sickness and suffering that is in our world
5. The expulsion from the garden
6. The pain that was to come with child-bearing
7. The corruption of the human heart
8. The loss of conditional immortality
9. The curse of the earth
10. The death of all humanity

Of course, all was not lost to Mother Eve, and correspondingly to all humanity. Eve fell, but in mercy, God held out the promise of a seed who would be born in the generations to come. The seed would provide the possibility of Eve's redemption and that of her generation. Genesis 3:15 states it thus:

> And I will put enmity
> Between you and the woman,
> And between your seed and her Seed;
> He shall bruise your head,
> And you shall bruise His heel

A patriarchal reading of the promise in Romans 5:1, 15-18 is stated thus by the Apostle Paul:

> Therefore, just as through one man sin entered the world, and death through sin, and thus death spread to all men because all sinned... For if by the one man's offense many died, much more the grace of

God and the gift by the grace of the one Man, Jesus Christ, abounded to many. ¹⁶ And the gift *is* not like *that which came* through the one who sinned. For the judgment *which came* from one *offense resulted* in condemnation, but the free gift *which came* from many offenses *resulted* in justification. ¹⁷ For if by the one man's offense death reigned through the one, much more those who receive abundance of grace and of the gift of righteousness will reign in life through the One, Jesus Christ.) ¹⁸ Therefore, as through one man's offense *judgment came* to all men, resulting in condemnation, even so through one Man's righteous act *the free gift came* to all men, resulting in justification of life.

The reality is that although Eve would face the sad moment of life even as she watched her vagabond son Cain murder his righteous brother, Abel, she was also able to see the rise of a second generation of the righteous through her son Seth. Ultimately, the promise made to her as recorded in Genesis 3:15, would be fulfilled in the coming of Jesus Christ. What can be said of her is that she fell, but got up again. Her rise shows the possibility of resiliency for women and men alike. A repeated line from the chorus of popular contemporary Christian songs says:

> We fall down, we get up.
> We fall down, we get up.
> We fall down, we get up.

There is a big lesson here. Failure might overtake us in life, but failure does not mean I am a failure. Failure at one moment does not mean the failure of my whole life. Failure does not define me. I need to learn lessons from my failure and move on to a life of opportunities that ever stands before me.

Reflecting on the discussion

1. What new insights that you have gained from the discussion?

2. Has there been any experience you faced that could have turned into defeat, but, by God's grace, has turned into a triumph?

3. Write a blessing that you desire for today, and for which you need to pray.

THE DAUGHTERS OF MEN

²² And as for Zillah, she also bore Tubal-Cain, an instructor of every craftsman in bronze and iron. And the sister of Tubal-Cain *was* Naamah. ⁴ There were giants on the earth in those days, and also afterward when the sons of God came in to the daughters of men, and they bore *children* to them. Those *were* the mighty men who *were* of old, men of renown.

- **Genesis 4:22; 6:4 NKJV**

THE DAUGHTERS OF MEN

As accusations spread against men concerning their egregious sexual actions against women, it is a fact of interest to reflect on one of Scripture's hardest passages found in Genesis 6:1-4. The passage reads:

> Now it came to pass, when men began to multiply on the face of the earth, and daughters were born to them, [2] that the sons of God saw the daughters of men, that they *were* beautiful; and they took wives for themselves of all whom they chose. [3] And the Lord said, "My Spirit shall not strive with man forever, for he *is* indeed flesh; yet his days shall be one hundred and twenty years." [4] There were giants on the earth in those days, and also afterward, when the sons of God came in to the daughters of men, and they bore *children* to them. Those *were* the mighty men who *were* of old, men of renown. (NKJV).

The varied interpretations of the passage are sometimes quite interesting. Here are three of them.

1. The most outrageous yet quite popular is the view that to build a superior race of humanity, angels of God (who some have argued were the sons of God) came to earth and had sexual intercourse with the daughters of men, and produced superbeings called Nephilim - used in Genesis 6:4.

2. A view that is less popular, but accepted by Bible scholars who argue from a covenantal perspective, is that the sons of Seth, the third son of Eve, who followed the way of the covenant, took the daughters of Cain, who were idolaters, as wives and had children with them.

3. The third view is that many of the faithful sons of God became enthralled with the daughters of men and decided to marry them, creating a corrupt race - a people who engaged in so much wickedness that God had to bring the judgment of the flood against them and saved only Noah and his family in the ark. In effect, what God pronounced as a blessing, the multiplication of the race (Genesis 1:28), became a curse, through mixed marriages.

After disposing of the most fanciful of the interpretations, which argues that angels had sexual intercourse with the daughters of men to build a super race of people, we need to give attention to the fact that the passage is pointing us to some severe concepts concerning the divine expectations for God's people.

Most notable in the passage is the fact that mix marriages between individuals who do not share similar religious or spiritual convictions have profound negative consequences for generations. As Israel was to settle in Canaan, God instructed them, "Do not intermarry with them [that is, the people of the land]. Do not give your daughters to their sons or take their daughters for your sons, [4] for they will turn your children away from following me to serve other gods, and the Lord's anger will burn against you and will quickly destroy you." (Deuteronomy 7:3,4 NIV). In the New Testament, the instruction is the same to the children of God, "Do not be yoked together with unbelievers. For what do righteousness and wickedness have in common? Or what fellowship can light have with darkness?" (2 Corinthians 6:14).

If the Old Testament passages were written in the contemporary age, it would probably read, "the daughters of God are marrying the sons of men." Maybe, the word marriage would not even be introduced since many women, as well as men, are using their freedoms to live in varied forms of relationships not sanctioned by God.

The point is that, although the Me Too Movement is challenging the sexual indiscretions of men, it also needs to challenge the sexual improprieties of women. Too many women are engaging in indiscriminate relationships that they have initiated. They have not set boundaries for purity and high moral integrity. Like many men, they are abandoning their spiritual blessings to satisfy their lustful passions.

In Matthew 24:37-39, Jesus predicted what is happening today. He said, "But as the days of Noah *were,* so also will the coming of the Son of Man be.[38] For as in the days before the flood, they were eating and drinking, marrying and giving in marriage, until the day that Noah entered the ark, [39] and did not know until the flood came and took them all away, so also will the coming of the Son of Man be." (NKJV)

Women, even though your fathers might be wicked and ungodly men, it does not mean that your life is lost and gone forever, or that you are destined for destruction. When God made you, he had a plan for your salvation. You can arise from the dust of any cruel, abusive, or rebellious situation to be called a daughter of God.

Reflecting on the discussion

1. What new insights that you have gained from the discussion?

2. Has there been any experience you faced that could have turned into defeat, but, by the grace of God, turned into a triumph?

3. Write a blessing that you desire for today, and for which you need to pray.

WOMEN IN THE ARK

⁷ So Noah, with his sons, his wife, and his sons' wives, went into the ark because of the waters of the flood.

- Genesis 7:7 NKJV

WOMEN IN THE ARK

One hundred and eighteen women have been elected to the United States Congress for the first time in history. The women claimed that they desire to help "save" the nation during its time of crisis. Interestingly, the crises are exacerbated by the more than 30 days of a partial government shutdown. These women see the suffering and want to help in changing the tragic conditions. It is my view that they can help. Historically, the salvation of families and nations have always needed the hands, not only of men but of women. In this, we must understand that men and women are not in competition.

The story of Noah and his wife is illustrative of how women can participate in the work of salvation. We read it in Genesis 6:18 that God said to Noah, "But I will establish my covenant with you, and you shall come into the ark, you, your sons, your wife, and your sons' wives with you" (ESV). Further, "The Lord … said to Noah, "Go into the ark, you and your whole family because I have found you righteous in this generation" … "And Noah did all that the Lord commanded him. Noah was six hundred years old when the floodwaters came on the earth. And Noah and his sons and his wife and his sons' wives entered the ark to escape the waters of the flood... In the six hundredth year of Noah's life, on the seventeenth day of the second month—on that day all the springs of the great deep burst forth, and the floodgates of the heavens were opened… And rain fell on the earth forty days and forty nights. On that very day

Noah and his sons, Shem, Ham, and Japheth, together with his wife and the wives of his three sons, entered the ark. (Genesis 7:1, 7, 11-13 NIV)

We have no details in the Bible concerning the name or the influence of Noah's wife or the wives of his sons. Jewish tradition says that Noah's wife, supposedly named Naamah, was a Cainite. The tradition also states that she was most beautiful. Whatever the truth of the tradition, the fact of interest is that Noah's wife and the wives of his sons were very much involved in the salvation of the world. Unlike the many women who were lost with their families in the flood, Noah's wife and her three daughters in law were women of great faith. The faith of these women, along with Noah and his sons, was tested during the building of the Ark. People ridiculed Noah for building a floating boat when rain had never fallen on the earth before. Their faith was also tested when Noah and his family entered the Ark, and for seven days, no rain had fallen. They must have waited anxiously and patiently, in the end, their faith triumphed. They were quite different from Lot's wife of whom we read later in the book of Genesis. On leaving Sodom, Mrs. Lot looked back, thus losing her faith and her life. She became a pillar of salt. (Genesis 19:26).

After the flood, the earth was repopulated by Mrs. Noah and her daughters in law along with their husbands. We often think that all humans came from the original man and woman - Adam and Eve, but how often do we ponder the fact that all post-flood living human beings are also descendants of Noah and his wife, and their three sons and their wives. When Paul declared that God "made of one [person] every nation of men to dwell on all the face of the earth" (Acts 17:26), he focused on Adam and Eve. But we must not forget that after the flood, it was the four women along with their husbands that repopulated the earth.

How surprised Noah's wife and the other three women might be if they were alive to see the struggles that have developed in the social order between gender and race. They would be glad to remind us that our competing interests will take us away into the flood. They would also say that since all humans descended from the eight people on the ark, we are one family. And, we need to say thanks for the faith of Mrs. Noah and her daughters in law, and their husbands. They have blessed the world. Without their faith, all humanity might have been destroyed.

In the history of humanity, women have always been a part of the story of salvation. They have been leaders. They have been exemplary and influential. They have prayed. They have faithfully shared their means that blessed the lives of millions. We shall reflect more on this, as we pursue the lives of other biblical women, but for now, the point is that we are not to forget that the wives who entered the ark had a significant part in the work of the world's salvation.

In our present crises, when the social and spiritual orders of our culture are being destroyed, we need more self-denying women, who will take their places where God leads them. We need them to help those who are seeking salvation in an Ark of safety, as did Noah's wife and her daughters in law. Yes, the world needs more authentic women to deal with our current crises.

Reflecting on the discussion

1. What new insights that you have gained from the discussion?

2. Has there been any experience you faced that might have turned into defeat, but, by God's grace has turned into triumph?

3. Write a blessing that you desire for today, and for which you need to pray.

A WOMAN UNDER PRESSURE

¹¹ And it came to pass, when he was close to entering Egypt, that he said to Sarai, his wife, "Indeed I know that you *are* a woman of beautiful countenance. ¹² Therefore it will happen, when the Egyptians see you, that they will say, 'This *is* his wife,' and they will kill me, but they will let you live. ¹³ Please say you *are* my sister, that it may be well with me for your sake, and that I may live because of you."

- Genesis 12:11-13 NKJV

A WOMAN UNDER PRESSURE

I do not know that I can join the crowd of those who like to call a certain White House Press Secretary, "a blatant liar." I felt pity for that individual when speaking on behalf of those who kept changing their stories. The Secretary didn't admit to giving the best information at the time, whether it was only a part of the truth or none at all. Her efforts to communicate what she was told reminds me of how women can sometimes be drawn into lying for powerful men.

I think of Sarai, the wife of Abram, on their way to Egypt. She was pulled into a plan to lie for the supposed protection of someone. According to what we read in Genesis 12:10-20, because of famine in the land of Canaan, Abram (later called Abraham) and Sarai (later be named Sarah) had to go to Egypt. Along the way, Abram looked at Sarai and noted her beauty and thought that Pharaoh, one of those powerful men who loved beautiful women, would likely have taken her away. Abram told Sarai that to save his life, she should not say she was his wife, but his sister. Abram and Sarai, planned to deceive Pharaoh, and it partly worked, for as soon as they reached Egypt, Pharaoh took Sarai into his harem. Of course, God intervened and attacked Pharaoh and his household with plagues, so that Pharaoh came to learn that he had done wrong in taking Abram's wife. He called Abram, apologized, and sent him away with riches.

The story of Abraham and Sarah telling their "half-truth" is repeated in Genesis 20, when they went to Gerar, the land of Abimelech, to escape another famine in Canaan. They heard that Abimelech would look for the most beautiful women in the nation and take them into his harem, to be his prospective wives. So, again, Abraham told Sarah to say she was his sister. The truth is that she was his father's daughter- his half-sister. On reaching Gerar, as mentioned before, Abimelech saw Sarah, and she told the half-truth once again. The result, Abimelech took Sarah into his harem. Again, God intervened, by allowing Abimelech to know the full truth in a dream that he had Abraham's wife in his harem, and that if he touched her, he would receive just due for his lack of integrity. Abimelech called Abraham, got him to admit his deception, and chided him. Abimelech pleaded his integrity, asked Abraham to pray God for him, and finally gave him gifts.

As we have seen, it was wrong for Sarah to join with Abraham to lie, but God, through his goodness, protected them. Of course, some questions of interest might be raised, for example, (1) How often do women get caught lying (or telling half-truths) for powerful men? (2) Why do some women lie for powerful men?

Here are some answers for your reflection. The responses are grounded in the context of the stories above but placed in our contemporary frame. Hopefully, they give insights into why some women participate in lying for powerful men.

1. Women lie for men because they **fear** them.
2. Women lie for men because they are **under profound pressure**.

3. Women lie for men because they believe **they are protecting themselves.**
4. Women lie for men because they are trying **to impress someone.**
5. Women lie for men because they are **participating in a cover-up.**
6. Women lie for men because they are **not fully trusting the Lord to protect them.**

Lest, as a reader, you are tempted to think only of Sarah or some other women lying, let me remind you that it is easy to tell lies when you are fearful, or under pressure or caught in circumstances that are difficult to negotiate. If you are thinking of Sarah, the wife of Abraham, or some other women, just ask yourself these questions:

1. How do I react when I am under pressure?
2. How do I respond when I am placed under challenging circumstances?
3. How do I behave in the presence of influential people?
4. Am I my true self, or do I pretend to be someone else?

Yes, remember that God is willing to intervene, but by telling that lie – that half-truth- Sarah put herself at risk. The truth is that lying will always place us at risk. Those who lie often have to keep on lying to cover up and protect themselves.

Be careful of lying, for as the Bible says: "Lying lips *are* an abomination to the Lord,

But those who deal truthfully *are* His delight." (Proverbs 12:22 NKJV).

Reflecting on the discussion

1. What new insights that you have gained from the discussion?

2. Has there been any experience you faced that could have turned into defeat, but, by God's grace, turned into a triumph?

3. Write a blessing that you desire for today, and for which you need to pray.

REMEMBER LOT'S WIFE

But Lot's wife, from behind him, [foolishly, longingly] looked [back toward Sodom in an act of disobedience], and she [a]became a pillar of salt.

— **Genesis 19:26**

REMEMBER LOT'S WIFE

Many surveys on religion in American, conclude that there is a dramatic decline in religious interest, not only among men but among women as well. About 35% of the population declare themselves as *Nones* - not having any particular religious' affiliation. Among younger Americans - Millennials and Gen Xers, the *Nones* are even higher, with 43-44 percent declaring that they are unaffiliated. Interestingly, the*re* are many women among the Nones.

What has brought about the non-connection to religion? While many are arguing that the fault is with the hypocritical attitude of religious folks, I see the issue as being more complex. I find a connection with the attitude identified in Lot's wife, found in Genesis 19. The Lord commanded her, along with her husband Lot, to get out of Sodom. However, on her way out, she got distracted, "looked back" and became a pillar of salt. (Genesis 19:26). What happened to her might seem trivial, but it was severe enough that Jesus referenced it when he was reminding his disciples that anyone who wished to follow him should focus on the forward direction and not look back as the wife of Lot, who "became that pillar of salt." Jesus framed it potently and dramatically when he said, "Remember Lot's wife." (Luke 17:32).

One might ask why Mrs. Lot received such drastic divine action and such forceful commentary from Jesus. Here are eight points that I offer as answers in a contemporary way:

1. Lot's wife was a materialist – Worldly things meant more to her than salvation.

2. Lot's wife was a consumerist – She had many imaginary wants - full of lust for vain things

3. Lot's wife was a socialite – She was making her friends and family, who were left behind, more important than God. Jesus warned that anyone who loved family and friends more than he is not worthy of him or the kingdom.

4. Lot's wife was a nominalist – She had religion, but it was superficial and idolatrous. Her religion lacked depth and commitment to God.

5. Lot's wife was self-centered – She lacked a spirit of self-denial and self-sacrifice. She was unwilling to give up things for God. It would have been good for her to hear the words of Jesus, "Seek first the kingdom of God and his righteousness and all things will be added to you" (Matthew 6:33).

6. Lot's wife lacked focus. She looked back, got distracted from the direction she was to go, lost her sense of purpose, and became frozen like a pillar of salt.

7. Lot's wife was double-minded. She was trying to serve two masters, as it were. In the words of Jesus again, "No one putting his hand to the plow and looking back is fit for the kingdom of God." One "cannot serve God and mammon" (Matt. 6:24).

8. Lot's wife got "ensnared" by the city lights of Sodom. She loved the pleasures that had surrounded her.

Yes, no one should doubt that it must have been hard to leave. However, when God says, "Get out" of a place, or a situation, "hasten for your life," it is crucial to listen to God instead of listening to the voices of the demons that are always calling. It is easy to put all the blame upon Husband Lot or some other person that might be a distracter, but each of us has a responsibility to ourselves. As we are told, we are to "Draw near to God, and he will draw near to you. Cleanse your hands, you sinners, and purify your hearts, you double-minded (James 4:8).

The following quotes that I have gathered from one of my most loved spiritual writers encapsulate the solid advice to those who are easily distracted. "Let nothing absorb your mind or affection or divert you from God." "Cast out every idol from your soul's temple." I have said to others, "Trust God's leadership in faith and follow him."

"Remember Lot's wife." Don't look back. Don't spend time regretting those things that are left behind. Leave them alone and focus on the kingdom as your destination.

Reflecting on the discussion

1. What new insights that you have gained from the discussion?
2. Has there been any experience you faced that could have turned into defeat, but, by God's grace, turned into a triumph?

3. Write a blessing that you desire for today, and for which you need to pray.

LOT'S DAUGHTERS

Then the men said to Lot, "Have you anyone else here? Son-in-law, your sons, your daughters, and whomever you have in the city—take *them* out of this place! ¹³ For we will destroy this place, because the outcry against them has grown great before the face of the Lord, and the Lord has sent us to destroy it."

¹⁴ So Lot went out and spoke to his sons-in-law, who had married his daughters, and said, "Get up, get out of this place; for the Lord will destroy this city!" But to his sons-in-law, he seemed to be joking.

¹⁵ When the morning dawned, the angels urged Lot to hurry, saying, "Arise, take your wife and your two daughters who are here, lest you be consumed in the punishment of the city." ¹⁶ And while he lingered, the men took hold of his hand, his wife's hand, and the hands of his two daughters, the Lord being merciful to him, and they brought him out and set him outside the city.

- **Genesis 19:12-16 NKJV**

LOT'S DAUGHTERS

We are at the moment in world history that calls for deep reflection on what might happen when parents make bad decisions that leave their children open to destruction. It might be a decision about leaving a child in a car, such as was noted on the front page of *USA Today*. As the story was reported, fifteen children died from being left in hot cars within a short period. The decision might also be to live in a place that makes one's child/ren vulnerable to rape victims or gun crimes. Or it might be to put a daughter or son in a place where false ideas of freedom make a rebel of the child. One poor choice by parents can put children in an unhealthy situation, and they are trapped.

In contemplating the above story, Lot's daughters readily come to mind. The biblical account in Genesis 19, speaks about Lot, his wife, and their daughters. The narrative begins with the arrival of two angels in Sodom. They were commissioned to bring destruction to the city. But Lot sees them in the street, and being a hospitable man, invites them to his house. That night a mob of men from the city surrounded Lot's house and demanded that he allows them to have sexual relations with his guests. To show hospitality to his guest, Lot makes a knee jerk decision and offers his two virgin daughters, who were at home, to the mob. The mob refused and made it clear that they were only interested in the visitors. The angelic visitors pushed Lot away from the door and blinded the men so that they were forced to cease their attack.

After the attack by the men of Sodom, the angels shared their mission with Lot and advised him that if he had other relatives apart from those in the immediate household, he should go and warn them to leave the city, because it would soon be destroyed. Lot left and went to warn his daughters and sons in law. However, they laughed at him and refused to leave the city. According to one commentator, "Lot returned sorrowfully to his home and told the story of his failure. Then the angels bade him arise and take his wife and the two daughters who were yet in his house and leave the city. But Lot delayed." The biblical record is that the command given to Lot was, "Flee for your life! Do not look behind you, nor stop anywhere in the Plain; flee to the hills, lest you be swept away." (Genesis 19:17). However, some of Lot's daughters clung to Sodom, and his wife refused to depart without them. The thought of leaving those whom she held dearest on earth seemed more than they could bear. It was hard to forsake their luxurious home and all the wealth acquired by the labors of their whole life, to become destitute wanderers. They were so confounded with sorrow that they lingered, wishing that they would not have to depart. Without the angels of God, they would all have perished in the ruin of Sodom. The angels took Lot, his wife and daughters by the hand and led them out of the city. (See, Ellen White, comments in *Patriarchs and Prophets*, 160).

This story is very riveting to read. Some people dismiss it as fiction, but it is of interest that when we press it, we can identify with how difficult it must have been for the family of Lot to leave two daughters (and two sons-in-law) in Sodom. No matter what mistakes they made as parents in establishing their house in Sodom, when they saw the possibility for their daughters' destruction, it was tough for them to leave. Yes, their daughters (and sons in law) were adults and had the right to refuse their invitation. However, being adults did not make it easier for them as parents to see their daughters (or sons-in-law) going to destruction while walking away without being burdened and broken in heart.

My wife and I listen to the burdens of many parents, and we see the brokenness all the time in our couples and parenting education classes in different settings. We hear the stories of the resistance and rebellion of many sons and daughters. Amid the stories, sometimes there is a giveaway when parents make an unintentional revelation, which makes it clear to us that the resistance and rebellion were inspired by something that they, the parents, had done. There is no need to make up stories. While we know of many innocent parents, we find that most parents are not as honest as they pretend to be. They wish to see their daughters and sons saved from "the sudden destruction that is about to come upon them." However, they do not want to start with confession and repentance; they want to begin with blame. They want to pass the buck to their daughters and sons. Also, yes, as the children become adults, they must take their part of the blame, but what we often see is that the problem is not just with the children, but with the parents, as well.

We need not belabor the latter point, concerning who is to blame. The point in this reflection is about the daughters of Lot and the great responsibility that fell upon Lot. Many commentators have noted that Lot did not take note of the corrupting influence the city was having on his daughters. Had he been more careful, he would not have chosen Sodom as a home. However, what he saw was the glimmer and gilts of the city, and he chose it. Further, if he and his family had not lingered, when told to "flee," his wife's heart might not have rested so much on their daughters in the city, and on her house, she was leaving behind. In the end, Mrs. Lot might not have become "a pillar of salt." (Genesis 19:26). If Lot had not gone to live in the city of Zoar, which was soon to be destroyed like Sodom, he would not have had to rush to the cave where they became so isolated that his two daughters, who left Sodom with him, made him drunk and had sexual intercourse with him. It was the encounter that produced the two nations of the Moabites and the Ammonites that became among two of the most idolatrous nations on earth and the enemies of Israel. As is said, "the curse of Sodom" followed Lot and his two daughters.

Let us raise the following six hard questions at the end of this reflection that might cause us to personalize the story of Lot's daughters more effectively. Some of the questions might seem rather preposterous, but in my view, they can lead to deeper reflection.

1. Is there a time when, despite one's burdened heart, one must leave their child/ren to make their own decisions for their salvation?

2. What does one do when one's daughter (or one's son) is under threat from an enemy, such as was the case with Lot's daughters and the mob at the door?

3. Is there a circumstance under which one needs to offer up one's (virgin) daughter/s to be gang-raped? Some mothers have done this for the sake of drugs.

4. How much care should parents give when choosing a home, especially when they have daughters (and sons, as well)?

5. What should parents do when they see their child/ren mirroring their own resistance, resentment, and rebellion?

6. If one has made a wrong decision concerning one's family, what might such a person do to correct the situation, especially when it seems that disaster is imminent?

Reflecting on the discussion

1. What new insights that you have gained from the discussion?

2. Has there been any experience you faced that could have turned into defeat, but, by God's grace turned into a triumph?

3. Write a blessing that you desire for today, and for which you need to pray.

DEALING WITH DELAY

And the Lord visited Sarah as He had said, and the Lord did for Sarah as He had spoken. **2** For Sarah conceived and bore Abraham a son in his old age, at the set time of which God had spoken to him. **3** And Abraham called the name of his son, who was born to him—whom Sarah bore to him—Isaac.[a] **4** Then Abraham circumcised his son Isaac when he was eight days old, as God had commanded him. **5** Now Abraham was one hundred years old when his son Isaac was born to him. **6** And Sarah said, "God has [b]made me laugh, *and* all who hear will laugh with me." **7** She also said, "Who would have said to Abraham that Sarah would nurse children? For I have borne *him* a son in his old age."

– **Genesis 21:1-7 NKJV.**

DEALING WITH DELAY

Have you ever had to wait on the Lord for anything in your life? How long have you had to wait for the fulfillment of a dream? In your book, how would ten years feel for the fulfillment of a dream? Have you ever had to wait for "Mr. Right" to come along? Or have you ever had to wait to birth a child, because you thought that you could not have a child? Were you tired of waiting, so you went out and adopted a child? Upon completing the adoption, something happened - you became pregnant. If you can say yes to the latter question, let me remind you that for some people who have waited long, things never work out as precisely. They waited and became so frustrated that they constructed their scheme to fulfill their desires. Yes, it might not be about pregnancy or marriage, but if you are honest with yourself, you can think of situations in which you lost your patience in waiting and did your own thing, assuming that all will be well. In the end, it did not work out the way you anticipated.

What has happened to you happened to Sarah, the wife of Abraham. Abraham was called the father of the faithful, and Sarah can be called the mother of the faithful. But as is evident, just like Abraham, Sarah's faith struggled for a while. When she was 74 years old, God gave Abraham the promise that he was to become the father of a great nation (Genesis 12). The promise was repeated in Genesis 17:16 that "Sarah would be the mother of nations" and conceive and bear a son. But, by then, it was hard for Sarah to believe. Time had passed. Now, after waiting ten years from the time of the promise, Sarah became so frustrated that she concocted a scheme. She suggested to Abraham that he should take her Egyptian maid, Hagar, and have a child with her. The plan was in keeping with the custom of the time. According to the culture, even adopted by the Rabbis, after 10 years, if a man had a wife and she was barren, she could give her maid as a surrogate, and when the child was born, she could take the child as her own.

Of course, the scheme did not work out well, because after Hagar became pregnant, she became so arrogant, that resentment developed in Sarah's heart, to the extent that she began to blame Abraham for Hagar's attitude. Abraham left it up to Sarah to solve the problem. And Sarah used the opportunity to abuse Hagar so severely, that Hagar ran away. (Cf. Genesis 16:1-6). More will be said about Hagar and divine intervention in a follow-up reflection, but for now, we return to the fact that 15 more years would pass before Sarah would give birth to Isaac, the promised child.

When Isaac was born, Sarah was 99 years old. She named her child Isaac, meaning "laughter," for she was thrilled. (cf Genesis 21:1-7). Of course, that was not the last time that Sarah's faith would be tested, for she had not yet dealt with her resentment. According to what we read in Genesis 21:9-11, "And Sarah saw the son of Hagar the Egyptian, whom she had borne to Abraham, scoffing. [10] Therefore she said to Abraham, 'Cast out this bondwoman and her son; for the son of this bondwoman shall not be heir with my son, *namely* with Isaac.' [11] And the matter was very displeasing in Abraham's sight because of his son." Yes, while we might not congratulate Sarah concerning her resentment, we need to see her from a human plain. She had waited long for a son, and to see him being mocked by his older brother was hard. Even mothers who have not waited so long for a child can be exasperated when their child is engaged in "rough play." I have seen them all the time. It demands a lot of faith and patience to grow children in the most normal of circumstances.

But let us get back to Sarah, for she sets up some of the most crucial questions about faith, for all of us. Here are seven that we might ask ourselves:

1. How do we react when we have to wait upon the Lord, 10, 15, 20, 25 years, and so on?
2. How well do we cope with delays?
3. What happens to our faith when we face dire situations in our lives?
4. Do we lose hope in the promises of God when we have an interval between promise and fulfillment?
5. In our "microwave," "social media," culture, are we willing to wait upon God for anything?
6. Are we willing to allow God's plans to work for us, or are we tempted to create our own "short shrift" plans?
7. Do we get in a panic when things are not working out as we would hope, or do we worry ourselves to death?

Can you identify with the above questions? If you are as I am, I am sure you can cry out with me, "Oh God help me through the difficulties of this life."

Reflecting on the discussion

1. What new insights have you gained from the discussion?

2. When you face situations in your life that could lead to defeat, how might you handle such experiences?

3. Write a blessing that you desire for today, and for which you need to pray.

SARAH'S ADVICE

Now Sarai, Abram's wife, had borne him no *children*. And she had an Egyptian maidservant whose name was Hagar. ² So Sarai said to Abram, "See now, the Lord has restrained me from bearing *children*. Please, go in to my maid; perhaps I shall obtain children by her." And Abram heeded.

- **Genesis 16:1, 2 NKJV**

SARAH'S ADVICE

The reality that Abraham took advice from Sarah has been a fact of great interest for many persons in our contemporary generation. They are uncomfortable with the point that is made when just after the fall, God said to Eve, "Yet your desire shall be for your husband, and he shall rule over you" (Gen. 3:16). This instruction has been seen by many persons as part of the burden which sin brought upon women. The instruction has been viewed by many persons as a command that women are to submit to their husbands. Some have said, it is a prescription, while others say it was a description (of what would have been). It is of significance that after the prescription or description that the next major husband and wife relationship in Scripture illustrates the wife's submission to her husband's rule. In this vein, it is argued that Sarah called Abraham, her husband, "lord" (Genesis 18:12). This was Sarah's way of expressing her submissiveness to Abraham. In the New Testament, Sarah is commended twice, once for her faith (Heb. 11:11) and the other for her submission to her husband (1 Pet. 3:5, 6). The Apostle Peter notes that Sarah "obeyed Abraham, calling him lord."

But we are not to miss the point that Abraham also submitted himself to Sarah, more than once. He submitted when he took her advice to take Hagar as a second wife (Genesis 16:3) and submitted again when Sarah became angry and requested that he should get rid of the slave girl from the home (Genesis 21:10). Abraham and Sarah evidently understood what the Bible teaches as "mutual submission." Some persons have argued that it is a myth that the Bible should call for mutual submission, as in Ephesians 5:21, "submitting to one another out of reverence for Christ." To such persons, "mutual submission" diminishes the role of authority in the home.

We are not to enter into what might be considered a frivolous debate here, we just find it interesting that Abraham should take the advice he did from Sarah. Sarah advised Abraham to take his maid Hagar as his wife and bear children with her. We do not know how Abraham felt, but we do know that he graciously complied. I have heard of a few women in our Western culture telling their husbands who to marry as a death bed wish, but I know of the practice that women in Middle Eastern, African, and Eastern cultures will introduce younger women to their husbands while yet alive. As acceptable as the practice is, there is proof that a new person in the home often creates marital conflict, as is the case between the Hagar and Sarah and Abraham and Sarah. There will be further discussions on how some of the conflicts have been resolved in other reflections. Here our observation is to state (1) that we need to be careful when we give advice and (2) that we are also to be cautious of the advice that we take.

Abraham listened to Sarah's advice, and it had a real deleterious consequence. Not all advice is good. If an advice goes against the will of God or is against the principle of right, we are to be careful that we give such advice or take such advice. What Peter and the apostles, who were arrested and taken to trial before the Sanhedrin said, is still relevant in any situation, "We are to obey God rather than human beings" (Acts 5:29).

Often enough, our faith might be challenged like that of Sarah and Abraham. How might we react? For a moment, the faith of Sarah became weak. She was just about running out of patience. Instead of bolstering Abraham's faith, she gave him, what Scripture records as "bad advice." Abraham thought by following the advice from his wife, he was going to fulfill the promise of God concerning his heir. It was the wrong choice.

If Sarah might be blamed for giving bad advice, Abraham might be blamed for taking bad advice. Thank God that despite the poor advice, God was able to redirect the way of Sarah and Abraham, so that in the years to come they would receive the fulfillment of the promise that God had intended for them.

The observation leads me to say that we are never to let any failure in our lives destroy our destiny, or chill our spirit. In fact, we are never to listen to advice from others that tells us to give up. Keep your passion for what you are seeking to attain. Have patience. Trust in God and ask for guidance to the end for which you are called.

Reflecting on the discussion

1. What new insights that you have gained from the discussion?

2. Have you faced challenges that could have turned into defeat, but for the grace of God?

3. Write a blessing that you desire for today, and for which you need to pray.

A FAVOR FOR THE UNFAVORED

⁷ Now the Angel of the Lord found her by a spring of water in the wilderness, by the spring on the way to Shur. ⁸ And He said, "Hagar, Sarai's maid, where have you come from, and where are you going?"

She said, "I am fleeing from the presence of my mistress Sarai."

⁹ The Angel of the Lord said to her, "Return to your mistress, and submit yourself under her hand." ¹⁰ Then the Angel of the Lord said to her, "I will multiply your descendants exceedingly so that they shall not be counted for multitude." ¹¹ And the Angel of the Lord said to her:

"Behold, you *are* with child,

And you shall bear a son.

You shall call his name Ishmael,

Because the Lord has heard your affliction.

Genesis 16:7-11 NKJV

A FAVOR FOR THE UNFAVORED

Have you ever been caught into a situation that you did not orchestrate? Someone who had power over you made a suggestion that you followed, and then you found yourself amid abuse and suffering and did not know what to do at the moment to get out? Yes, it is true that if you had thought more carefully, would you have walked away before you followed the instruction. Or would you take some blame for allowing a moment of weakness to overtake you and to get you trapped? Would you say you want to walk away, but you are in, and you are more confused than ever, you do not know what to do?

If such has ever happened to you, I want you to relate what happened to Hagar. According to what we read in Genesis 16:1-16, Hagar was an Egyptian servant (slave) in Abraham's and Sarah's house. Tradition has it that she was one of Pharaoh's daughters given over to Abraham for Pharaoh offense in taking Sarah, Abraham's wife, into his harem. In returning Sarah to Abraham, and sending them away, Pharaoh gave Hagar to them as a servant. After Abraham and Sarah waited some ten years for the heir that God had promised them, Abraham and Sarah became bewildered – their faith became weak. Thus, Sarah told Abraham to take Hagar as a wife (or concubine, as some translations have it). Abraham followed the suggestion, and Hagar went along. Hagar became pregnant, and, of course, was as "proud" of her pregnancy as many women would be. Her pride awakened the jealous rage of Sarah so much that Sarah turned on Abraham and blamed him for the trouble that he caused in her house. After Abraham reminded Sarah that Hagar was her slave, Sarah began to "mistreat" Hagar to the extent that Hagar ran away. The Lord found Hagar in the desert and sought to comfort her. Here is the touching encounter in Genesis 16:8-16 (NIV):

> The angel of the Lord found Hagar near a spring in the desert; it was the spring that is beside the road to Shur. [8] And he said, "Hagar, slave of Sarai, where have you come from, and where are you going?"
>
> > "I'm running away from my mistress Sarai," she answered.
> >
> > [9] Then the angel of the Lord told her, "Go back to your mistress and submit to her." [10] The angel added, "I will increase your descendants so much that they will be too numerous to count."
> >
> > [11] The angel of the Lord also said to her:
> > "You are now pregnant
> >   and you will give birth to a son.
> > You shall name him Ishmael,
> >   for the Lord has heard of your misery.
> > [12] He will be a wild donkey of a man;
> >   his hand will be against everyone
> >   and everyone's hand against him,
> > and he will live in hostility
> >   toward all his brothers."

¹³ She gave this name to the Lord who spoke to her: "You are the God who sees me," for she said, "I have now seen the One who sees me." ¹⁴ That is why the well was called Beer Lahai Roi; it is still there, between Kadesh and Bered. ¹⁵ So Hagar bore Abram a son, and Abram gave the name Ishmael to the son she had borne. ¹⁶ Abram was eighty-six years old when Hagar bore him Ishmael.

Hagar's encounter with the Lord is insightful. It was not all comforting, but a deeper reflection shows that it was transformative. Her son would face difficult times in life. He would have to struggle against the many evil forces that he would encounter. But what the Lord did was comforting enough to the heart of any young woman so bound up with distress.

In fact, if, for any reason, you made a mistake with your life and come to a place where you feel sore and distressed, I invite you to call on the Lord. As the chorus of Peter Bilhorn's 1891 song reminds us:

> *The best friend to have is Jesus,*
> *He will help you when you fall,*
> *He will hear you when you call;*
> *The best friend to have is Jesus*

Reflecting on the discussion

1. What new insights that you have gained from the discussion?

2. Have you ever faced any experience in life that might have been a defeat, but for the grace of God?

3. Write a blessing that you desire for today, and for which you need to pray.

RESENTMENT IS NOT THE SOLUTION

But God said to Abraham, "Do not let it be displeasing in your sight because of the lad or because of your bondwoman. Whatever Sarah has said to you, listen to her voice; for in Isaac, your seed shall be called.

– Genesis 21:12 NKJV.

RESENTMENT IS NOT THE SOLUTION

Have you ever done something that you regretted? Did your action put you in trouble? And did you become angry, not just at yourself, but at God, as if it were God's fault? Or have you ever become resentful at someone you know, like a friend, who seems more successful than you? Or have you ever become resentful at someone who has children and you don't? Have you been resentful because you have children, and the children are demanding so much of you that you would wish to be freed from them like your friend who has none? Have you ever wanted to go somewhere and you could not go because of the children?

Resentment is a strange problem. You might be surprised, but it arises in the best of human beings. We struggle with it and try to hide it. We hate to admit it. And it remains in the breast and grows and grows until it bursts out as a chronic problem that kills its host. Some persons do not suffer from resentment as a chronic illness, but it might come to them as one who has caught a cold from time to time. It just creeps up at them for reasons that they cannot explain. Yes, it is something strange that is very difficult to explain, but it is present, and it spoils the character.

Yes, resentment is found in many places. We see it in spousal relationships. It is common in sibling relationships. It anchors itself among friends and colleagues at work. It is visible among church members. When one can sing and the other cannot, it shows its ugly head. When one can speak well and the other cannot, it appears. When one has many gifts, and another does not, it is present. When one gets a lot of attention, and the other does not, it is persistent, it plays out. The eight most common reasons for resentment are identifiable as:

1. Power – I want your power
2. Privilege – I want your privilege
3. Position – I want your position
4. Possessions – I want your belongings
5. Popularity – I want fame
6. Profession – I am jealous of you, because of your professional accomplishments
7. Pain – I have been hurt by you, and I have a lot of pain.
8. Poverty – I do not want to associate with you because you are too poor.

Have you ever thought of how one of the greatest matriarchs of history suffered from resentment? After being married to Abraham for many years, Sarah did not have a child – she was barren. So at a moment when she was most fearful at the prospect of not having a child, she panicked and did something quite foolish. She encouraged Abraham to go to bed with Hagar, her helper so that she would become the surrogate mother. However, when Hagar became pregnant, Sarah became resentful. The resentment was not only toward Hagar but also Abraham. The resentment grew and grew until Sarah began to abuse Hagar to the extent that Hagar ran away. On the way to Shur, the Angel of the Lord found Hagar by a spring of water in the wilderness, inquired where was she from, and where she was going. Hagar responded, "I am fleeing from the presence of my mistress Sarai." The angel recognized the danger in which she was in the wilderness and said to her, "Return to your mistress, and submit yourself under her hand." (Genesis 16:8-9).

It was a hard choice, but Hagar returned. A little later, Sarah conceived and bore Isaac, but the resentment continued to grow in her heart until Hagar's son was about sixteen years old. One day as Sarah saw her son, Isaac, and Hagar's son, Ishmael, engaging in "rough play" Sarah got so angry that she demanded that Abraham should throw out Hagar and her son. Abraham did, and from then, a wall of separation was built between the off-springs of Sarah and those of Hagar, until this day.

Sarah is known as one of the greatest matriarchs in the covenant line, despite her resentful attitude toward Hagar. But such resentment must not be trivialized. In fact, the Bible does not downplay resentment but shows the shadow it casts over Sarah's home. We are told that resentment opens the heart to the devil. It poisons the soul. It messes up the mind. It breaks forth into anger, bitterness, hatred, and finally, violence. Unless a resentful attitude is acknowledged, confessed, and jettisoned from the heart, it will eventually kill its host.

Yes, resentment is one of the most destructive sins. It is very insidious, and unless it is destroyed, it will ruin any heart in which it lives. To remove resentment from the heart, one needs to become vulnerable, humble, reasonable, patient, and forgiving. One must ask God to take away the spirit of pride, possessiveness, protectiveness, and evil passions that are at the source of resentment.

Kill resentment, or it will kill you.

Reflecting on the discussion

1. What new insights that you have gained from the discussion?

2. Are there experiences you have had that could have been a defeat, but by the grace of God, you were victorious?

3. Write a blessing that you desire for today, and for which you need to pray.

RETURNING TO AN OPPRESSIVE SITUATION

"Return to your mistress, and submit to her"

– **Genesis 16:9**

RETURNING TO AN OPPRESSIVE SITUATION

How should one who is facing a situation of oppression, such as sexual abuse, physical abuse, or psychological abuse, respond? Should such a person accept the situation, as the will of God for him/her to suffer in such a way? This reflection might be profoundly interesting to you as a reader, especially if you were married and needed counsel after being abused. You went to your pastor about what was happening to you, and the pastor told you it might be God's will for you to stay in the situation. Or you might be on the job being treated unjustly, and when you complained to a trusted friend, the friend reminded you that, as a Godly person, you were called to suffer the hurt that your job is causing you.

I worked in a situation similar to the last reference named above while in graduate school. For one year, I worked in a bakery in Michigan. Each day that I went to work, the manager gave me a big pile of mixing bowls and other utensils to wash. Sometimes it seemed the dish pile would get larger and larger. I went to work each day for that year, but day after day I felt the resentment building up in my heart, especially because my mates who went to work with me were given opportunities to help with baking, operating the slicing machine or doing other tasks that seemed more honorable than mine. I felt that the duties given were assigned according to complexion. Toward the end of the school year, I told the manager that I would not be returning after my summer break. He told me how great a worker I was and how much he would miss me. I said goodbye and left. I did not want to hear anything else from him. I was glad to know that the job had provided the help needed to cover my expenses for the school year. But if someone had come along to tell me that God was expecting me to go back, I would have thought them crazy. Or maybe I would have put a "curse" on them.

In thinking of the work scenario above, I have often wondered why when Hagar ran away from the abusive treatment of her mistress, Sarah, and she cried to God from her hiding place in the wilderness, God told her to "return to her mistress" (cf. Genesis 16:6).

It seems a strange thing what God did. God told Hagar to return to her mistress. Was it God? The Bible says it was. This acknowledgment leads me to ask, "Did God take pleasure in Hagar's suffering? Did God want her to return to her situation of oppression, instead of going to find the freedom that she might have found if she could have reached Egypt? I am not trying to complicate the question but rather show that what might seem a contradiction might come by divine direction because there are challenges in our world of contradictions that only God understands. For instance, being out there in the wilderness allowed Hagar to be extremely vulnerable. She might have been exposed to predators who would rape her, as is happening in many situations in our world today. Places, where such is occurring, is not in the wilderness, but in homes and workplaces. In spite of what was possible in Egypt, Hagar was safer in Sarah's house. Although the Bible does not tell us that we must always go back home to abuse and oppression, it tells us that God instructed Hagar on this occasion to go back home.

Of course, the text does not stop with the command to go back home. Instead, it shows how God gave Hagar a great (re) assurance of blessings:

> The Angel of the Lord said to her, "Return to your mistress, and submit yourself under her hand." [10] Then the Angel of the Lord said to her, "I will multiply your descendants exceedingly so that they shall not be counted for multitude." [11] And the Angel of the Lord said to her:
>
> "Behold, you *are* with child,
> And you shall bear a son.
> You shall call his name [d]Ishmael,
> Because the Lord has heard your affliction.
> [12] He shall be a wild man;
> His hand *shall be* against every man,
> And every man's hand against him.
> And he shall dwell in the presence of all his brethren."
>
> [13] Then she called the name of the Lord who spoke to her, You-Are-the-God-Who-Sees; for she said, "Have I also here seen Him who sees me?" [14] Therefore the well was called Beer Lahai Roi; observe, *it is* between Kadesh and Bered. (Genesis 16:9-14 NKJV).

Wow! "Out of evil comes forth [some] good" for in returning home, not only was there safety for Hagar, but there was protection for her child. It gave time for her son, Ishmael, to bond with his father, Abraham. Returning gave Hagar and her son time to learn about the covenant God, instead of going to Egypt, where they would have been implanted in the culture of the Egyptian gods. Indeed, just as Hagar had life's lessons to learn from events in her life, so might we also learn.

Sometimes we might not be able to know what God is doing in our situation, but we can trust his care that he will not "leave us or forsake us." In some other translations, it says that he will not leave us as orphans, or without comfort (John 14:18), but he will come to us, and be with us in our times of trouble.

You can take comfort that he is taking care of you.

Reflecting on the discussion

1. What new insights that you have gained from the discussion?

2. What situations have you face in life that could have been disastrous but, for the grace of God?

3. Write a blessing that you desire for today, and for which you need to pray.

THE GOD WHO SEES

"She gave this name to the LORD who spoke to her: 'You are the God who sees me,' for she said, 'I have now seen the One who sees me.'" ... She said, 'You are the God who sees me.' She also said, 'Have I truly seen the One who sees me?'"

- Genesis 16:13, NIV.

THE GOD WHO SEES

Have you ever felt like you were trapped in a maze, a *cul de sac*, or in the midst of a wilderness? Have you ever been passing through some of the most trying experiences and before you reached the depth of the conflictual situation, you tried to explain to family and friends, the complexity of your condition? Do they listen but seem not to have a clue as to how you are feeling? Worse yet, when you call on God, did you feel as if He stepped out on you? He is gone into hiding (Psalm 88:14)? "Is God gone to sleep," as the Psalmist contemplated (Psalm 7:6; 35:23; 77:7; 78:65)? Here is how the Psalmist felt when he wondered if God had gone to sleep. In Psalm 44:23, he shouts, "Awake, Lord! Why do you sleep? Rouse yourself!" And to such deep anguish God responds, "For the oppression of the poor, for the sighing of the needy, **Now I will arise**," says the Lord; "I will set *him* in the safety for which he yearns." (Psalm 12:5 NKJV, emphasis mine).

Hagar, Sarah's maid, felt a deep and compassionate response from God, when she was in her trial in the wilderness. When she called on the name of the Lord, and He spoke to her, she recognized who he was and acknowledged him by saying, You-Are-**the-God-Who-Sees**; "Have I also here seen Him who sees me?" (Genesis 16:13 NKJV). It was not a coincidence that the well by which Hagar sat was appropriately called Beer *Lahai Roi* (Genesis 16:14), meaning *the God who sees*.

What profound comfort these words from God brought to Hagar, who had been abused by her mistress? The comfort she felt can be ours today. It is a joy to know that God is **The All-Seeing God**. He is wide awake. He sees us in our times of trouble. He knows our feeble frame – our fears, our worry, our hurts, our temptations, our suffering, our pain, our loneliness, and all of our painful conditions. Again, the Psalmist tells us, "Behold, He who keeps Israel Shall neither slumber nor sleep." (Psalm 121:4 NKJV). Humanity sleeps. We all can go for a few days without sleep, but we all know that sleep deprivation causes trouble in our brains and other body systems. In fact, sleep deprivation causes spiritual confusion. The gods that many humans worship are asleep. It is believed that some of the gods sleep in the winter and awaken in the spring or summer. The God whom Hagar met, never sleeps. The Eternal God never slumbers and never sleeps. He is the holy watcher, who sees what we do and hears what we say, all the time.

We do not know at what point Hagar shared her encounter with God, but one might suspect that as soon as she returned to Abraham and Sarah, she told them about the manifestation. She made it clear that the God who sees, saved her unborn child, and that he was merciful in saving her life, too. We might settle it that Hagar was deserving of some of the treatment that Sarah meted out to her was deserving because of her arrogance about her pregnancy. When Hagar found herself pregnant for Abraham, while Sarah was barren, she mocked Sarah. And Sarah, who was not willing to accept such disrespect from her maid, turned on her. Hagar got what she deserved, we might say. Or we might say it was the divine judgment against her. When my grandmother raised her hands to heaven, and said, "God is not sleeping," she was saying that the divine is going to bring judgment against anyone who contended with her. Thank God, Grandma did not always get her desire, for God sees differently than how human beings see. He sees the heart of each person and knows the depth of their pain.

In effect, we need to be thankful that God does not want to treat us as we deserve. Through his mercy, he saves us. As the Apostle Paul says, "[It is] not because of righteous things we had done, but because of his mercy. He saved us through the washing of rebirth and renewal by the Holy Spirit" (Titus 3:5 NIV). Just as God manifested himself to Hagar and she revived and was able to tell her story, so God will reveal himself to us, if we will let him, so that we can tell our stories.

When we see God, we need to tell of his mercies. When God works on our behalf, we are to testify. When God saves us, we are to spread the news. When God comforts us, we are to bring a smile on our faces. We are to tell it, not only for our contemporaries but, like Hagar, we are to share it with the next generation. We might not name a well, like Hagar, but we need to find a way to put on the memorial wall of our lives what God has done. We are to tell so that future generations might use our story to see that our God is a God who cares.

Sometimes, of course, God chastens us. He uses the harsh moments of our lives to humble us, not humiliate us. He uses the harshness to shape our characters. He uses suffering to build our endurance. When we have understood what God is doing with us, we will be able to name the place where we meet him, Beer *Lahai Roi – the God who sees.*

He sees. He cares. And we can trust him. Ask yourself, how do you respond to God's care? Do you appreciate it? Do you rejoice in it? Have you cast yourself upon him, knowing that he cares for you? (1 Peter 5:7).

Reflecting on the discussion

1. What new insights that you have gained from the discussion?

2. Have you had any experience that might have turned into defeat, but for the grace of God?

3. Write a blessing that you desire for today, and for which you need to pray.

SARAH AND THE SACRIFICE OF ISAAC

So Abraham rose early in the morning and saddled his donkey, and took two of his young men with him, and Isaac his son; and he split the wood for the burnt offering, and arose and went to the place of which God had told him.

- **Genesis 22:3 NKJV**

SARAH AND THE SACRIFICE OF ISAAC

After reading Genesis 22 and taking note of the sacrifice of Isaac by Abraham, it is always hard for me to leave the chapter without asking several questions, namely:

> Where was Sarah on the night when Abraham left the house with Isaac?
>
> Why did not Abraham awaken Sarah if she was in the house and asleep?
>
> What happened when Sarah awoke and did not see Abraham and Isaac in the house?
>
> Where is Sarah's voice in the story?

The Bible does not answer the questions directly, but some commentators have suggested that the burden upon Abraham's heart, for offering the son of his inheritance on Mount Moriah, was so heavy that he did not dare share the request with Sarah. Knowing Sarah's love for her son, for whom she had waited all these years, Abraham knew that Sarah would have pressed upon him to preserve Isaac's life. He knew that pressure from his wife, Sarah, might have caused him to change his mind. Other commentators suggest that after the divine intervention, and Abraham returned from Moriah with Isaac, that Abraham stopped, and for a while settled in Beersheba (Genesis 22:19), and very likely Isaac went home to Kiriath Arba, which is Hebron. Isaac might have shared the news of what took place with Sarah, and it sickened her so much that she died (Genesis 23:2). Abraham then went home to eulogize Sarah and to mourn for her. He bought a piece of land and buried her.

The Rabbis have all kinds of exciting shades of interpretation for the story. There is no need to repeat them here. No one should try to be dogmatic about what really happened. What is quite clear is that Sarah loved Isaac. Sarah was very connected to Isaac. She even became irate when she felt his half-brother, Ishmael was mocking him. Her commitment to guard Isaac would have allowed her to stay up all night to watch if she knew that Abraham was going to take him away from home. Of course, Sarah respected Abraham. She also knew Abraham's love for Isaac and would do nothing to harm him. She had high regard for God and would not allow herself to think that God would ask anything inappropriate of her or Abraham. This is why the New Testament gives so much affirmation to Sarah's faith. Note the following three texts, for example:

1. Hebrews 11:11, 12 NKJV "By faith, Sarah herself also received strength to conceive seed, and she bore a child when she was past the age because she judged Him faithful who had promised. [12] Therefore from one man, and him as good as dead, were born *as many* as the stars of the sky in multitude—innumerable as the sand which is by the seashore.

2. 1 Peter 3:6 NKJV "as Sarah obeyed Abraham, calling him lord, whose daughters you are if you do good and are not afraid with any terror.

3. Galatians 4:21-22 NIV [22] For it is written that Abraham had two sons, one by the slave woman and the other by the free woman. [23] His son by the slave woman was born according to the flesh, but his son by the free woman was born as the result of a divine promise.

What an example is Sarah? Thanks to God that there are many mothers today, who are as faithful as Sarah was. Before, and upon her death, we have heard the Bush family talk of Mother Barbara's love, dedication, and commitment. My father gives much credit for the salvation of his children to his wife - our mother, Mary. However, it is painful to note that many mothers these days are sacrificing their children on idolatrous altars. Many are neglecting the care of their children. If you are reading this reflection, in whatever you do, I want you to think of Sarah. If you lived in her home, you could have a real sense of security, for she would do all she could to protect you.

Reflecting on the discussion

1. What new insights that you have gained from the discussion?

2. Has there been any experience you that could have turned into defeat, but, for the grace of God?

3. Write a blessing that you desire for today, and for which you need to pray.

THE DEATH OF SARAH

So Sarah died in Kirjath Arba (that *is*, Hebron) in the land of Canaan, and Abraham came to mourn for Sarah and to weep for her.

- Genesis 23:2 NKJV

THE DEATH OF SARAH

In our contemporary culture, public mourning is not the norm. Often, we are suffering a lot of grief, but we are suppressing it. No wonder that there are anxieties and depression in many lives. In contrast, I think of the death of Sarah and how Abraham mourned for her loss. The biblical text states, "Sarah lived to be a hundred and twenty-seven years old. She died at Kiriath Arba (that is, Hebron) in the land of Canaan, and Abraham went to mourn for Sarah and to weep over her." (Genesis 23:1-2 NIV). Despite his mistakes of exposing Sarah to danger when he asked her to lie, there is no question that Abraham loved Sarah. After mourning for his wife and preparing a fitting burial, Abraham reconstructed his life.

In contrast, Scripture passes over Isaac's reaction to Sarah's death. There is silence. We are not told that he took part in his mother's burial or in mourning, as observed by his father. Isaac is not even mentioned in Genesis 23. Of course, we can learn something about Isaac's emotional reaction to his mother's death indirectly, from the account of his marriage to Rebekah in Genesis 24:67. It says, "Isaac then brought her [Rebekah] into the tent of his mother Sarah, and he took Rebekah as his wife. Isaac loved her and thus found comfort after his mother's death" (Gen. 24:67). Evidently, Isaac grieved over his mother's death a long time and went through the complexity of the emotional process that impacts most humans. But when he took Rebekah, he was comforted for Sarah.

I do not know if, as you read this reflection, you can identify with Abraham or Isaac concerning Sarah's death. What I know is that a mother's death causes deep pain. My mother died at the age of 96, and my mother-in-law at 95 ½. Both had reached a stage of life where there was no quality of life. Each was compromised in their health conditions, in the latter days of their lives. We hated to see them suffer, and when they died, we were relieved they were free from pain and suffering. Since they were both faithful Christians, our beliefs lead us to think of the text in Revelation concerning the blessing on the saints who die in the Lord, "Then I heard a voice from heaven saying to me, "Write: 'Blessed *are* the dead who die in the Lord from now on.'" "Yes," says the Spirit, "that they may rest from their labors, and their works follow them." (Revelation 14:13 NKJV). Of course, the fact that we were relieved, does not say that we did not mourn our losses. After attending the funerals and singing the songs of hope, we returned home, and for days on ending and even years, we have felt the pain, and I often hear myself saying, in *soto voce*, "My mom is gone." I also note the same with my spouse; I hear in undertones, "My mom is gone."

The loss of a mother is something that one never seems to overcome, no matter how old one gets. In fact, my dad has outlived mom by eight years. In his 105th year, I still hear him saying towards the end of every phone call I make to him, "Your mom was a great woman." He ends his sentences with, "I really miss her."

Abraham moved on, and Isaac moved on. My Dad has had to move on. And my spouse and I, and all our siblings have had to move on. While we have moved on, memories of the great lives of our mothers have not been erased. The pain is not entirely removed. What we have accepted is that in this world, the loss of mothers and fathers, and even children will come. Several things can be done to help a person move on. Abraham, for example, married Keturah, and Isaac married Rebekah. Some individuals have children to take the place of the lost. Others attend a grief support group. Others get involved in creative tasks. Some travel. Some move in to live with love ones. Others engage in compassionate services - they reach out to others. There are several beneficial approaches to healing. Some people even try insignificant things to erase the painful memory. While I do not endorse trivial strategies, each one must find something that can be effective in reorienting the profound depth of the separation and pain.

Among the most useful things that one can do, however, is to act like Abraham and other individuals of faith. Through the centuries, they sought to "Look for the city which has foundations, whose builder and maker *is* God." (Hebrews 11:10 NKJV).

Might I ask you, How are you dealing with your grief and pain? Do you have both a temporal solution and an eternal plan?

Reflecting on the discussion

1. What new insights that you have gained from the discussion?

2. Has there been any experience you encountered, that could have turned into defeat, but for the grace of God?

3. Write a blessing that you desire for today, and for which you need to pray.

THE INFLUENCE OF A MATRIARCH

Now it came to pass after these things that it was told Abraham, saying, "Indeed Milcah also has borne children to your brother Nahor: [21] Huz his firstborn, Buz his brother, Kemuel the father of Aram, [22] Chesed, Hazo, Pildash, Jidlaph, and Bethuel." [23] And Bethuel begot Rebekah. These eight Milcah bore to Nahor, Abraham's brother. [24] His concubine, whose name was Reumah, also bore Tebah, Gaham, Thahash, and Maachah.

– Genesis 22:20-24 NKJV

THE INFLUENCE OF A MATRIARCH

When Mrs. Barbara Bush passed away, she was eulogized in many ways, with the highest compliment noting that she was considered one of the most powerful matriarchs to have been in America's public life. Although many individuals in the Women's Liberation Movement had sought to trivialize her work as a mother, Barbara Bush resisted their criticism, while she insisted that motherhood was to be seen as the most praiseworthy and respected role of women in the world. After much opposition from students who felt that a woman who emphasized her motherhood, Barbara Bush was invited to give the Commencement Address at Wellesley College (in Massachusetts), on June 1, 1990. In 1999 her address was rated on a list of 47 among the best speeches of the century. Upon her death, Barbara Bush was spoken of in laudable terms about her positive influence on her family and families in her generation. She was the wife of a president, the mother of a president, and the mother of a governor. Her other children and grandchildren have noted their blessing as a result of her life.

The work of many women, as mothers, have been much more obscure, than Barbara Bush's, but one should not deny their powerful influence. When I think of a woman like Milcah, I think of a mother who evidently lived in obscurity, but who, in my view, has a most profound influence on her grand-daughter. Here is how the Bible profiles Milcah:

> Now it came to pass after these things that it was told Abraham, saying, "Indeed Milcah also has borne children to your brother Nahor: 21 Huz his firstborn, Buz his brother, Kemuel the father of Aram, 22 Chesed, Hazo, Pildash, Jidlaph, and Bethuel." 23 And Bethuel begot Rebekah. These eight Milcah bore to Nahor, Abraham's brother. 24 His concubine, whose name was Reumah, also bore Tebah, Gaham, Thahash, and Maachah. –Genesis 22:20-24 NKJV

What is stated about Milcah is that she was the mother of eight sons she bore to Nahor, the brother of Abraham. What is known in a connected story is that when Abraham was seeking a wife for his son Isaac, he sent his servant Eliezer to Aram to find someone from his own family. It is quite evident that Abraham had confidence in the faith of his family. It was different from the religion of the Canaanites or Moabites from whom his elder son Ishmael had taken a wife. So, Abraham wanted a wife for Isaac for his clan, who evidently had knowledge of the true God. Whatever part Milcah played in sustaining the family's faith, we cannot be dogmatic, but we can surmise that she wielded a very strong powerful influence as mothers and grand-mothers sometimes do.

Milcah was the grandmother of Rebekah. And in today's world, we might not think of the grandmother's far-reaching influence, but in traditional societies, where the extended family was close together, a grandmother had as much impact, if not more than some mothers. In fact, those who can identify with certain conditions in our modern world, where many grandmothers have to be rearing their grandchildren, will appreciate my argument that it is not far-fetched to think that Milcah likely had a positive influence on Rebekah.

As stated, we cannot be dogmatic about Milcah, but we can laud the influence of obscure mothers and grandmothers who sacrificed their lives for the blessing of their children. Yes, might I say, your influence counts. We can write many books on the power of a mother's/grandmother's influence and the extent of their impact through generations. Just think of the following:

1. The atmosphere that mothers and grandmothers create about their homes.
2. The wholesome (or unwholesome) attitude that they display.
3. The stories of the generations that they share with their children.
4. The values that they communicate.
5. The trust (or distrust) that they help to build.
6. The love and affection that they transfer.
7. The religious fervor that is transmitted.

One can appreciate why king Asa of Judah removed his grandmother Maccah from her position as queen mother because she had made a detestable Asherah pole. According to 1 Kings 15:13, King Asa chopped down the pole and burned it in the Kidron Valley. My point is that we need to say to godly mothers and grandmothers, "Your positive influence has continued to carry your children and grandchildren in the world as it is. God bless each one of you, no matter how obscure you might think you are."

The most significant power that we have in our world is through the influence we wield in families. It is not the power of control; it's the power of influence. Godly mothers and grandmothers have helped to form the characters of many, and our world is made better for it. I, who have been abundantly blessed by a powerful mother, say, "Thank you."

Reflecting on the discussion

1. What new insights that you have gained from the discussion?

2. Has there been an experience you encountered that could have turned into defeat, but for the grace of God?

3. Write a blessing that you desire for today, and for which you need to pray.

THE RIGHT WOMAN FOR A WIFE

⁷ The Lord God of heaven, who took me from my father's house and from the land of my family, and who spoke to me and swore to me, saying, 'To your descendants I give this land,' He will send His angel before you, and you shall take a wife for my son from there. ⁸ And if the woman is not willing to follow you, then you will be released from this oath; only do not take my son back there."

- Genesis 24:7, 8 NKJV

THE RIGHT WOMAN FOR A WIFE

Some time ago, I had a discussion with a young man about his marital interest. He told me he had a checklist of some thirty items, and that he was waiting to find the woman who met all of the items on his list. Whoever met those qualifications would become his wife. I do not know "what planet he is from," as the saying goes, but what he said was quite mystifying. Not that I did not think men should not look for the right woman, but his list was what threw me. After such a baffling response, I paused to reflect on how many who are postponing marriage might have the same or similar reasons as the young man had. It is common knowledge that many young adults in the millennial generation are delaying marriage and having children later than previous generations. They are taking more time to get to know each other before tying the knot. Others are "shacking up" but are unwilling to make marital commitments.

The narrative above leads me to ask, "What are young men looking for in a woman?" "What are young women looking for in a man?" The answers would demand a complete essay, but we might use an ancient example to show that sometimes a person might not have a list, but seek the divine wisdom to find the appropriate partner. The story with which our questions are identifiable is recorded in Genesis 24. It tells of the efforts made to find a wife for Abraham's and Sarah's son, Isaac. When the time came for Isaac to be married, Abraham called his trusted servant, Eliezer, placed him under oath, and sent him to Padan Aram, to find the wife for his son. Abraham sent him to the household of Bethuel, who was the youngest son of his brother, Nahor, and his wife, Milcah. Bethuel had two children, Laban and Rebecca. Upon reaching Padan Aram, Eliezer stopped by a well and prayed this prayer:

> "O Lord God of my master Abraham, please give me success this day, and show kindness to my master Abraham. 13 Behold, here I stand by the well of water, and the daughters of the men of the city are coming out to draw water. Now let it be that the young woman to whom I say, 'Please let down your pitcher that I may drink,' and she says, 'Drink, and I will also give your camels a drink'—let her be the one You have appointed for Your servant Isaac. And by this, I will know that You have shown kindness to my master." (Genesis 12:12-14 NKJV).

The answer came quickly, for before Eliezer had finished speaking, a beautiful young lady came to the well to give her flock water. Eliezer asked her for a drink of water. She gave it to him and also told him that she would draw water for his camels also. Without hesitation, she diligently watered all of the camels. Eliezer, excited about the answer to his prayer after a brief conversation, recognized who she was, and in turn, told who he was. Eliezer then gave her a ring telling her that she was a prospect for his master's son. Rebecca, realizing that Eliezer was connected to her relative, took him home to meet her family. On reaching home, Eliezer told the family of his mission, and how the Lord had guided him. After consultation with the family, Rebecca consented and gladly went with Eliezer to meet and marry Isaac at Abraham's home.

For all else that is known concerning the relationship between Rebecca and Isaac, Rebecca seemed to have been the right wife for Isaac. She was not perfect, but she was the right wife. She brought balance to the life of Isaac. She compensated for his weaknesses. Did they have difficulty? Yes, they did, at least, in the way that they expressed their feelings for their twins, Jacob and Esau. Rebecca favoring Jacob and Isaac favoring Esau. Apart from this, one has to admire Rebecca. Eliezer took note that she was a beautiful bride. She was virtuous, in the sense of being a virgin. But beyond the physical, she also was a kind, courteous, patient, thoughtful, diligent, hardworking woman. She was clear about the divine will, and when she noticed that Isaac had evidently forgotten the divine intent for Jacob over Esau, she showed her wisdom in working out God's plan. Of course, the way she did it made it clear that when a human being tries to help out God, they make a mess of things.

Whatever else one might think, Rebecca was a wonderful wife for Isaac. She offered the correctives that he needed. Which is to say, while one might not find a wife from the kind of list that the young man mentioned in our opening paragraph, one can find the right wife if one is willing to depend on God to give the wisdom to choose, and knowledge to help along the way. A man (or a woman) should not depend on mere externals to select the kind of partner that one desires, but one must focus on the qualities of character evidenced in Rebecca. On a man's part, it is about finding the **right** wife. On a woman's part, it is about finding the **right** husband. Of course, one needs not be searching for a lifetime for Mrs. Right or Mr. Right, for there are many opportunities if one will learn of the divine wisdom what is right.

Reflecting on the discussion

1. What new insights that you have gained from the discussion?

2. Has there been an experience you faced that could have turned into defeat, but for the grace of God?

3. Write a blessing that you desire for today, and for which you need to pray.

SHE WILL BE GOOD FOR YOU

Our sister, *may* you *become the mother of* thousands of ten thousands; And may your descendants possess the gates of those who hate them."

— **Genesis 24:60 NKJV**

SHE WILL BE GOOD FOR YOU

If you had been following my life's story for many years, you would likely have heard or seen my many references about the question one of my college faculty mentors asked me. She was interested to know my feelings about the young lady whom she saw that I was showing some interest. After hearing my response, she said to me, "I think she will be good for you." "Good for me?" I mused. Anyone who knows me understands that such a suggestion would leave me in deep contemplation. I did get married to the very young lady about whom my mentor spoke. But I went back to my mentor about six times to clarify what she meant by "She (my wife) will be good for you" My mentor always responded with smiles, to my query. Maybe she did not know what to make of her intuition, other than what she later said, "I told you so. See, you and your wife are together for so many years [forty-nine actually]". What I know is that although my mentor's intuition was most powerful, I credit many more things, including the great blessings of God, that have held our lives together. After my mentor had given her affirmation, my parents, aunt, and sisters were also impressed and encouraged my choice.

How many persons, these days, are so blessed as I have been? I cannot say, but I am convinced that many could use some of the same kind of blessings and affirmation. My story leads me to think of the story of how Rebecca became the wife of Isaac. The full story is told in Genesis 24 and is quite lengthy, but here are some highlights:

- Abraham was getting quite old.

- Before his death, he wanted to see Isaac married to a wife who loved the Lord.

- He called his servant Eliezer who was in charge of his house to go get the wife for Isaac.

- He told Eliezer to go back to his homeland and family in Haran to find that right wife.

- Eliezer was willing to go but doubted that he would find the right woman and whether she would be willing to follow him back to Canaan.

- In sharing his fear, Abraham pressed back upon him, and he followed the instruction.

- Abraham required an oath by asking Eliezer to put his hand under Abraham's rib.

- Then he went on the journey.

- Along the way, he paused to pray that God would guide him.

- In the prayer, he asked God to show him the right person by a test.

- The test worked in a way that he was able to precisely identify who the Lord wanted him to meet.

- He asked her to take him to her home to meet her family.

- Upon her acceptance of the invitation, Eliezer blessed the Lord for his guidance and blessed Abraham for his insights. It was a successful find.

- After making acquaintance with the young lady who was identified as Rebecca, the granddaughter of Nahor, Abraham's brother, the servant requested to meet her family. On reaching home, Eliezer recited to Rebecca's family how God had blessed Abraham. Then he told of the mission on which he had been sent, the oath he took, the journey to the well where the women came to draw water for the animals, the prayer that he had prayed to find the wife for his master's son, Isaac, the providential meeting, the proposal offered to Rebecca, her acceptance of the plan, and the blessing (or worship) that he gave to God for the answering his prayer. Eliezer concluded with the request for Nahor and the family to endorse what God had done. The family approved Eliezer's story and conferred with Rebekah to see if she would go to Isaac and Abraham. Rebekah's family showed their delight at her fortune as follows: "And they blessed Rebekah and said to her: "Our sister, *may* you *become the mother of* thousands of ten thousands; And may your descendants possess the gates of those who hate them." (Genesis 24:60).

Although we might find the cultural mode of relationship formation quite anachronistic, yet we can learn multiple lessons from it. Such lessons will not be stated here because of space limitation; however, one might at least ask a few questions such as: What part does divine wisdom play in our mate selections today? Do we want to know what the will of God is? Do we listen to the impressions God gives in this regard? It is essential to state that many times, God sends us his affirmation through parents and many other intuitive individuals around us. Let us check carefully what He sends us, and we will be truly blessed.

God is ever willing to bless us and sustain us in all our relationships. Therefore, let us invite him into our decisions as we are to make them.

Reflecting on the discussion

1. What new insights that you have gained from the discussion?

2. Has there been an experience that you faced lately that might have turned into defeat, but for the grace of God?

3. Write a blessing that you desire for today, and for which you need to pray.

HELPING OUT GOD

⁵ Now Rebekah was listening when Isaac spoke to Esau, his son. And Esau went to the field to hunt game and to bring *it*. ⁶ So Rebekah spoke to Jacob, her son, saying, "Indeed I heard your father speak to Esau your brother, saying, ⁷ 'Bring me game and make [a]savory food for me, that I may eat it and bless you in the presence of the Lord before my death.' ⁸ Now therefore, my son, obey my voice according to what I command you. ⁹ Go now to the flock and bring me from there two choice kids of the goats, and I will make savory food from them for your father, such as he loves. ¹⁰ Then you shall take *it* to your father, that he may eat *it,* and that he may bless you before his death."

— **Genesis 27:5-10 NKJV**

HELPING OUT GOD

Humanity, through the generations, seems to be the same. We are always trying to help God accomplish his plans. Of course, in our effort, we find short cuts. We do not want to wait. Our patience seems, always, to run thin. What we want is to get responses by microwave or 5 G. We just cannot allow the answers to our prayers, "Thy will be done on earth as it is in heaven."

Remember Rebekah, the wife of Isaac, and what she did with the destiny that God had set forth for her sons? As the twins struggled in her womb, and she began to question what was going on, the Lord revealed to her that "The older would serve the younger."(Genesis 25:23). The backdrop to the story is that after Rebekah had waited for twenty years from the time of her marriage to Isaac to have a child, she found herself pregnant with twin sons, Jacob and Esau. Jacob was born last, but at his birth, he held on to the heel of Esau. Rebekah remembered the revelation and the incident of the delivery, and, undoubtedly, discussed it with Isaac many times. But Isaac was caught up in his culture and was determined to make Esau the child of his inheritance. Isaac found a way to allow Esau to know that he had the birthright and that he would have the blessing. It must have been a thing of interest to watch the competing agendas in the home, between Isaac and Rebecca. "Isaac loved Esau because of the venison which was to his taste, and Rebekah loved Jacob" (Genesis 25:28). As Isaac's eyesight began to fail, and he thought that his imminent death was at hand, he asked Esau to prepare venison for him after which, he would give Esau the final blessing of the inheritance. Rebekah overheard the instructions to Esau, and immediately, she planned to subvert Isaac's wish. She sought to ensure that Jacob would receive the blessing. Her plan for the moment was most effective. She prepared venison using a young goat, then used the goat's skin to wrap Jacob's neck and arms. She then encouraged Jacob to put on Esau's clothing. The "deception" was intended to make Jacob feel and smell like Esau and in turn, receive the blessing.

Yes, Rebekah was effective in helping to make the blessing go to the one for whom it was intended, but many questions remain.

1. Was Rebekah a deceiver or an inspired woman?
2. Did she allow her love for Jacob to rule her mind?
3. Did she allow her ambition to overrule her judgment?
4. Did she use her insight to take advantage of Isaac's blindness?
5. Did she allow herself to become a control freak?
6. Did she show integrity in what she did?
7. Did she allow her gentle spirit, which was first evident to be lost?

While we need to commend Rebekah, it is clear that some of her actions did not lead to a peaceful life at home. The communication between her and Isaac seemed to have broken down. The jealousy and resentment, for which she bears tremendous responsibility, between the two brothers, became so intense that murder was about to take place. In the end, Rebekah convinced Isaac that Jacob must be sent away to her brother Laban in Padan Aram, Syria. It is not clear, in the end, whether Jacob or

Esau hand the opportunity to attend Rebekah's funeral. The only note we have in Genesis is that when Jacob became old, and was about to die, he requested his sons in Egypt, where the family was now living, to take his body back to the cave of Machpelah, where Abraham, Sarah, Leah, and Rebekah were buried (Genesis 49:31).

Although Rebecca did not act with total integrity in carrying out God's plan, yet, it is of interest to note God's mercy. When the Apostle Paul argues for the fact of how God carried forward his promise to Israel, he takes note of how God used Rebekah as an instrument in the plan of election (See Romans 9).

What we might need to focus on here is not so much how Rebekah made mistakes in trying to carry out God's plan but to take note of her passion for the plan of action. Rebekah was anxious to do what was right. She was committed to it. In fact, she took quite a risk to make it happen.

The question for us, as we reflect on the life of Rebekah is, how passionate and committed are we about God's plans for our lives and that of those who are under our charge?

Reflecting on the discussion

1. What new insights that you have gained from the discussion?

2. Has there been any experience that you faced that could have turned into defeat, but for the grace of God?

3. Write a blessing that you desire for today, and for which you need to pray.

DOUBLE CROSSING A SISTER

Now Reuben went in the days of wheat harvest and found mandrakes in the field, and brought them to his mother, Leah. Then Rachel said to Leah, "Please give me *some* of your son's mandrakes." [15] But she said to her, "*Is it* a small matter that you have taken away my husband? Would you take away my son's mandrakes also?" And Rachel said, "Therefore, he will lie with you tonight for your son's mandrakes." [16] When Jacob came out of the field in the evening, Leah went out to meet him and said, "You must come in to me, for I have surely hired you with my son's mandrakes." And he lay with her that night

- **Genesis 30: 14-16 NKJV**

DOUBLE CROSSING A SISTER

How would you feel if you were Rachael? How would you feel if you had met a person that you saw as a life's partner? A person that you would like to have totally to yourself, as spousal relations are supposed to be? And then your best friend, or sister, comes and takes the person away? The behavior is called in common *lingua franca*, "double-crossing."

This is the story of Rachael. According to what we read in Genesis 29, she met Jacob by a well while he was running away from his angry brother Esau who wanted to kill. It was love at first sight. After sharing their story and finding out the familial connection, Rachael hastened home. She reported to her father, Laban, and the rest of the family that she had found a family member. Laban sent one of his sons to invite Jacob home. The family celebrated. Laban then assured Jacob that he could stay with the family. Jacob used the opportunity to make a proposal to request Rachael in marriage. He would work for seven years, in place of paying a dowry. All were in agreement, and Jacob worked his best for the seven years. But on the day of his prospective marriage to Rachael, things turned out badly. Laban decided, in agreement with Leah, the older sister, that she would be the bride, all unknown to Jacob.

In the morning, instead of his beautiful Racheal beside him, Jacob found Leah. He was outraged and immediately went to confront Laban. Laban explained to Jacob that it was the custom there. A younger sister could not be married before an older sister. But Jacob loved Rachael, so he proposed to Laban that he would work another seven years so that he could have her as a wife. Laban accepted the proposal, and so Jacob worked fourteen years to get the love of his life.

After the marriage of Jacob to Rachael, the bliss they anticipated was not realized. There was no joy or peace. From the switching of Leah for Racheal, a lot of jealousy, resentment, and even rage developed between the two sisters. Like a bad omen, after her marriage to Jacob, Rachael was barren for many years. Although Jacob reassured her of his love, her life was one of misery. Leah made her life even more miserable by finding several ways of flaunting her fertility. An unhealthy competition developed between the two sisters. It was so intense that each began to try in various ways to gain Jacob's attention. Rachael gave her servant to Jacob so that she could become a surrogate. When Racheal's maid began to have children, Jacob spent most nights with Rachael, and Leah complained that Rachael was stealing her man from her. Leah, in trying to fight back, gave her maid to Jacob so she could have more children.

The story became exciting when Ruben, Leah's eldest son, went into the fields and had a rear find of mandrakes, that beautiful flowering plant, believed to be an aphrodisiac. He brought the mandrakes home to his temporarily infertile mother. Leah thought that by allowing Jacob to know she had the mandrakes, she could tempt him to come and sleep with her, at least for one night. He went to sleep with her, and she became pregnant. When Leah got the mandrakes, Rachael showed her frustration and asked Leah to share some with her. The request intensified the competition between the two sisters to the extent that Leah brought the jealousy into the public as she challenged Rachael as the Scripture shows.

> Now Reuben went in the days of wheat harvest and found mandrakes in the field, and brought them to his mother, Leah. Then Rachel said to Leah, "Please give me *some* of your son's mandrakes." 15 But she said to her, "*Is it* a small matter that you have taken away my husband? Would you take away my son's mandrakes also?" And Rachel said, "Therefore, he will lie with you tonight for your son's mandrakes." 16 When Jacob came out of the field in the evening, Leah went out to meet him and said, "You must come in to me, for I have surely hired you with my son's mandrakes." And he lay with her that night (Genesis 30: 14-16 NKJV).

Leah did not give any of the mandrakes to Rachael, but Rachael was blessed otherwise as she saw that God had not forgotten her. After her many years of trying, she had her very own son, Joseph. Although she would not live to see it, Joseph was named among the greatest governors of Egypt and gave guidance to Pharaoh on how to survive seven years of famine. Joseph also became the savior for his family that would later go to live in Egypt. The two sons of Joseph - Ephraim and Manasseh- became tribal leaders in Israel. Upon her death bed, Rachael had a son whom she called Benoi, later named Benjamin, the father of the tribe from which the first king of Israel would be selected.

The point is that, as bad as things can get, all is not lost, especially when God is in charge. Sometimes a person's life can be profoundly harsh, but somewhere from the shadows, victory appears. Victory does not always come in one's lifetime, but sometimes after one's death.

Reflecting on the discussion

1. What new insights that you have gained from the discussion?

2. Has there been any experience you faced that could have turned into defeat, but for the grace of God?

3. Write a blessing that you desire for today, and for which you need to pray.

NOT SO BEAUTIFUL, BUT BLESSED

Then Laban said to Jacob, "Because you *are* my relative, should you, therefore, serve me for nothing? Tell me, what *should* your wages *be?*" ¹⁶ Now Laban had two daughters: the name of the elder *was* Leah, and the name of the younger *was* Rachel. ¹⁷ Leah's eyes *were* [b]delicate, but Rachel was beautiful of form and appearance.

– Genesis 29:15-17 NKJV

NOT SO BEAUTIFUL, BUT BLESSED

Have you ever been in a relationship that made you miserable? A relationship in which you did not feel that you were treated with the kind of affection that you expected? Have you ever been called ugly by one from whom you expected positive affirmation? Have you ever been thought of as less than you believe yourself to be? Have you ever been caught in a love triangle because of your naivety? Have you felt you should have taken some responsibility, but you were honestly caught in the situation, because someone who had so much power over you, imposed themselves upon you? And before you became conscious of it, you were up to your neck in the relationship? Although some persons are willful in their actions, there are situations when explained, might draw your sympathy.

In a culture where powerful men prey upon the vulnerability of women, it is not so naïve to think that such might not have been necessarily the case. No, I am not making excuses. There are multiple cases that I know, which, from my perspective, were at points of vulnerability where individuals got caught up in situations in which they might not otherwise have been. And while people look at them from the outside and make negative judgments, God looks at their case from the inside and offers them grace. Remember what the Lord said to the prophet Samuel when he went to anoint one of the sons of Jesse to be the next king of Israel: "But the Lord said to Samuel, "Do not look at his appearance or his physical stature, because I have refused him. For *the Lord does* not *see* as man sees; for man looks at the outward appearance, but the Lord looks at the heart." (1 Samuel 16:7 NKJV)

Do you remember Leah, I mean the sister of Rachael, of whom I wrote in a prior reflection? As part of that reflection, I noted that Rachael was beautiful and drew the attention of Jacob's eyes at first sight. Leah, who was forced upon Jacob as a first wife, was not so impressive. Some commentators argue that Leah had a "crocked" nose and "crossed" eyes. Other commentators say that the Hebrew name **Le'ah** meant "weary." Others say her name might be related to the Akkadian *littu* meaning "cow." What an insult if the name has such significance? If Leah's father, Laban, intended his first daughter's name to mean something positive, it turned out to be a challenge. Of course, Leah's most significant difficulty was not in her looks or her name. Her greatest challenge rested in the arrangement to force her upon Jacob as a first wife, in place of Rachael. From then on, she suffered much anger and resentment from Jacob. As we noted, in a previous reflection, her sister Rachael resented her with good reason.

It was not an easy life for Leah, as well as for Rachael. Two sisters caught up between one man, because of their father's indiscretion. One has to say, thanks be to God for grace and mercy. Sometimes in the mazes of life, we are caught up in such difficult situations that only God can get us out of there. A more in-depth look at Leah's experience makes clear that God's intervention transformed her miserable condition, to which she contributed. In spite of the polygamous marriage, she became the mother of six of Jacob's sons Ruben, Simeon, Levi, Judah, Issachar,

Zebulon, and his daughter Dinah. The names that Leah chose for her children revealed her piety and deep sense of obligation to the Lord. The intent here is not to elaborate on the meanings of the names of Leah's children, but to note that two of the sons, namely Levi and Judah, became dominant among the tribes of Israel. From Levi came Moses, the most powerful leader Israel ever knew, and through Aaron, the priesthood, was established. Through the tribe of Judah, the Davidic kingship was established and through which Jesus Christ was born.

The point made is that amid the most challenging situations of our lives, the God who guides the daily movement of the world does not forget us in our messy situations, that we sometimes help to create. God will do whatever is needful to offer us an opportunity for salvation. People might think our situation hopeless. They might call us "unpleasant" names. And we might find it hard to get out of the mess in which we find ourselves, but the good news is that God is watching.

Although the unattractive Leah might have repulsed others, God was attracted to her because of her inner beauty, which at times, it seemed, the lovely Rachel lacked. The renown commentator Abraham Kuyper has been quoted to say, "There is a beauty which God gives at birth, and which withers as a flower. And there is a beauty which God grants when by His grace men (sic) are born again. That kind of beauty never vanishes but blooms eternally." The point is that behind many an unattractive or unlikable face, there is a lovely disposition.

My appeal to women is simple. Whenever you are tempted to think of yourself as inadequate, as less than others, or as a put-My down, think of Leah. God lifted her and made her great. He can do the same for you.

Reflecting on the discussion

1. What new insights that you have gained from the discussion?

2. Has there been any experience you faced that could have turned into defeat, but for the grace of God?

3. Write a blessing that you desire for today, and for which you need to pray.

SITTING ON AN IDOL

And now you have surely gone because you greatly long for your father's house, *but* why did you steal my gods?" ³¹ Then Jacob answered and said to Laban, "Because I was afraid, for I said, 'Perhaps you would take your daughters from me by force.' ³² With whomever you find your gods, do not let him live. In the presence of our brethren, identify what I have of yours and take *it* with you." For Jacob did not know that Rachel had stolen them. ³³ And Laban went into Jacob's tent, into Leah's tent, and into the two maids' tents, but he did not find *them*. Then he went out of Leah's tent and entered Rachel's tent. ³⁴ Now Rachel had taken the [d]household idols, put them in the camel's saddle, and sat on them. And Laban [e]searched all about the tent but did not find *them*. ³⁵ And she said to her father, "Let it not displease my lord that I cannot rise before you, for the manner of women *is* with me." And he searched but did not find the [f]household idols.

- Genesis 31:30-35 NKJV

SITTING ON AN IDOL

Just because an investigation is completed and the investigated is declared innocent, might not be innocent before God. At times, even the one who has been declared innocent might not feel so. God knows the truth, and the one acquitted often knows the truth or falsehood of the declaration.

Remember Rachael, the one spoken of in the Bible? She was the daughter of Laban, sister of Leah, and the second wife of Jacob. In Genesis 31, we find the story of Rachael who sat on the "household idols" or teraphims that she had stolen from her father. Remember how Jacob and his two wives and their whole family were running away from the oppressive hands of Laban one night to go to Jacob's home, which he had left 21 years before in Palestine. "When Laban had gone to shear his sheep, Rachel stole her father's household gods." (Genesis 31:19). And the whole family left.

When Laban returned home and found out that Jacob had gone with his two daughters and his grandchildren and all his possessions for which Jacob had labored for the 21 years, Laban was furious. He got some of his servants to saddle the camel, and together they went after Jacob. When Laban caught up with Jacob, there was a great confrontation. After challenging Jacob about how he left, Laban accuses Jacob of stealing his household idols. Jacob protested and told Laban to search everywhere among his goods and to see if he could find the idols.

Jacob was unaware that Rachel had stolen the idols, and so he "Anyone with whom you find your gods shall not live. In the presence of our kinsmen point out what I have that is yours, and take it." (Genesis 31:32). It was a profoundly unwise comment from Jacob, but all of us in various ways can identify with him. Maybe we declared certain people innocent, such as our children or others who we trusted when, in truth, they were guilty. It's a good thing that Laban did not find the idols on which Rachael was sitting. The night ended relatively peaceful without any loss of life (read the rest of Genesis 31 for the details).

Yes, when Laban went to Rachael's tent, she was sitting on a stool. She apologized to Laban that it was the time of her period and that she could not arise. After his careful investigation, Laban never found the idols, for Rachael was sitting on them. When Laban left on his homeward journey, Jacob discovered, to his horror, that Rachael was sitting on the idols.

The Bible does not tell us why, but it only states that Rachael stole the idols. Several theories have been put forth why Rachael stole the idols. Here are three, I expand for clarity:

1. Rachel wanted to punish her father for the mean way in which he treated her husband and family. By taking the thing that he cherished most, she knew of the hurt she would cause him. "Serve him right," she might have said.

2. Some commentators suggest that Rachel disapproved of her father's (Laban's) idol worship and wanted to help prevent it. So she took them away.

3. The most plausible one I've heard was that Rachel was an idolater (idol-worshipper) herself. She was following family customs and traditions. Rachel must have known of Jacob's God. He must have told her of the vision he had at Bethel. He must have taught her that the God he served does not accept the worship or the making of idols (the first and second commandments, that would be repeated in codified form to Israel at Sinai). Yet it seems that Rachel's customs and tradition meant more to her than the commandments of God.

I am interested in the fact that Rachael sat on the idol because of one of the points that the Bible makes about idolatry. Idolatry is not only what we see in the external, like an image of Buddha, or the 3000 carved images that the Hindus worship, or the statues in Roman Catholic worship spaces, the window images in many homes, the crucifixes that are worn, the little trinkets that we place on our ears, or wear around our necks, our the motor cars that we drive and think that they are more important than God. But idolatry is also the hidden secrets in our hearts. In Ezekiel 14:1-8, the prophet Ezekiel was told that God could not bless some of the leaders of Israel, because they had "idols in their hearts." They were idol worshipers, but they were hiding their idols. They were conceited, being very deceptive, pretending to be religious, even spending their time in temple worship, but in their hearts, they had their idols. Some people will not admit the idolatry in the heart, so let me ask:

1. Are there idols in your minds? What about the worship of your ideas?

2. Are there idols in your flesh? What about the worship of your desires or your lusts, your worship of food or sex, or some other passions or vanities, that might be hidden for a while but will come to the public view, one day?

3. Are there idols in your spirit? What about your pride, your looks, or some other oppressive and depressive, burdensome image that you are carrying about?

I could ask about some of the other idols on which you might be sitting, but what I want to bring to the fore is that if you are an idol worshiper, God only has one request of you, stated in the imperative. 1 Corinthians 10:14 "Wherefore, my beloved, flee from idolatry" (1 Corinthians 10:14).

Reflecting on the discussion

1. What new insights that you have gained from the discussion?

2. Has there been any experience you faced that could have turned into defeat, but for the grace of God?

3. Write a blessing that you desire for today, and for which you need to pray.

THE DEATH OF A RIVAL SISTER

Then they journeyed from Bethel. And when there was but a little distance to go to Ephrath, Rachel labored *in childbirth,* and she had hard labor. ¹⁷ Now it came to pass, when she was in hard labor, that the midwife said to her, "Do not fear; you will have this son also." ¹⁸ And so it was, as her soul was departing (for she died), that she called his name [a]Ben-Oni; but his father called him [b]Benjamin. ¹⁹ So Rachel died and was buried on the way to Ephrath (that *is,* Bethlehem).

– Genesis 35:16-19 NKJV.

THE DEATH OF A RIVAL SISTER

In the last two weeks, four families, close to ours, lost loved ones. One friend who is in her mid-nineties, called as soon as it happened, to report that her sister had passed away. She wanted to see us and our first son, who is her god-son. She gave the impression that she wanted us to come quickly. When we went to see her, she never said why she wanted to see us so quickly, but we could feel a sense of appreciation for our presence. She just wanted to see her god-son, too. After we left, she kept calling until they were able to get together.

Yes, the death of a sister can be very distressing. Let's think of Rachael, the sister of Leah. We may not know how prophetic, but in his protest against Laban for charging him with stealing his idols, Jacob had declared, "Anyone with whom you find your gods shall not live. In the presence of our kinsmen point out what I have, that is yours, and take it." (Genesis 31:32). Wow! After Laban left without finding the idols, Jacob realized that Rachael had them. We are not sure about the lapse of time between Jacob's declaration and Rachael's death, but one could make the point that it might not have been very long after. Rachel died while giving birth to her second son, Benjamin (Benoni, as she named him). Have you ever wondered how Leah felt?

Leah and Rachael had lived their later lives as competitors. They often resented each other, as we understand it, calling each other "husband thief." But the death news must have brought Leah to a moment of deep reflection. She and Rachael had played together, laughed together, and maybe gotten in mischief together when they were children. Now, death had taken Rachael away. It was a time of questioning, sadness, anger, disbelief, despair, grief, and pain. Leah might even have felt guilty, that the constant struggle had allowed her "dear" sister Rachael to die so early. If Rachael had lived another day, they might have been able to work out their relationship much better instead of constantly blaming each other for what their father had done to them.

Although, at times, Leah might have wished Rachael dead, yet when Rachael died, the pain of separation must have been profound. Death has no consideration. It is cold. It takes away our loved ones. It makes us grieve. It makes us lonely. It makes some persons afraid to share in intimacy. It makes some feel a profound sense of rejection. It makes us all feel the sense of our vulnerability and mortality. To some, death brings the loss of hope.

In any situation, death is perplexing. Whether it happens suddenly or through sickness and over time, whether it happens to someone young or someone old, whether it happens by accident or by natural causes, through pregnancy or the birthing of a child, death is disconcerting. It might meet us along the road of life, as happened to Rachael. Rachael died along the way, in Ephrath (Genesis 35:16-18), from Padan Aram to Canaan. She did not get to live out her days, like Leah, or be buried in the cave beside Jacob (See Genesis 49:31).

One might think that in her death, Rachael would be forgotten, but she plays a prominent role in biblical prophecy. A thousand or so years after her death, Rachel is portrayed symbolically, by the prophet Jeremiah: "Thus says Jehovah: A voice is heard in Ramah, lamentation, and bitter weeping. Rachel weeping for her children; she refuses to be comforted for her children for they are not." Somehow she would be comforted. The Lord instructed her to refrain from her weeping for she would be rewarded, and "her children" would return from the land of the enemy (Jeremiah 31:15-17). She wept because her off-spring were taken into captivity. Joseph was the father of Ephraim and Manasseh, both of whom became prominent leaders in Israel (the northern kingdom), while Benjamin was with Judah (the southern kingdom). When the nation of Israel went into Assyrian captivity (722-21 B.C.), and the people of Judah (with the tribe of Benjamin) were carried into Babylonian captivity in 586 B.C, the prophet Jeremiah says that Rachael wept. The desolation was so heart-wrenching that it seemed that her children "were not," i.e., they were dead. And the prophecy speaks of her symbolic refusal to be comforted.

Later, when Jesus was born, and Herod heard through the Wise Men from the East (The Magi) that a new king was born in Israel, he slaughtered the children of Bethlehem. Thus, Matthew picked up the prophecy of Jeremiah by saying, "A cry was heard in Ramah--weeping and great mourning. Rachel weeps for her children, refusing to be comforted, for they are dead." (Matthew 2:18).

Enough has been said to make the point that sometimes we might lose a sister or a brother in death, and we think all is gone. But there is hope.

God has not forgotten the sister (or the brother). In effect, if you have lost a loved one, take heart, all is not lost. God remembers.

Reflecting on the discussion

1. What new insights that you have gained from the discussion?

2. Has there been any experience you faced that could have turned into defeat, but for the grace of God?

3. Write a blessing that you desire for today, and for which you need to pray.

THE TRAGEDY OF RAPE

One day Dinah, the daughter of Jacob and Leah, went to visit some of the Canaanite women. ² When Shechem son of Hamor the Hivite, who was chief of that region, saw her, he took her and raped her.

- **Genesis 34:1, 2 (GNT)**

THE TRAGEDY OF RAPE

Although the confirmation hearing of Judge Brett Kavanaugh, in the United States Congressional Committee, is now behind us, the scene might be still fresh in our memories. I continue to think how sad it would be if every woman who came forward to report a rape or some other form of sexual abuse were treated in the same disposable manner, like the ones in the hearing. However one might have judged the discussion, there has to be the agreement that the historical challenges women confront as victims of sexual harassment, abuse, and rape must be addressed with respect and fairness than has been the case in many forums.

Let us take a turn away from our contemporary frame where our personal biases and emotions might be blinding us to the realities of a rape victim, and let us consider the story told in the Bible concerning the rape of Dinah. It is a typical case of the treatment meted out to some rape victims. The story, as shown in Genesis 34, notes that Jacob was traveling back to Canaan from Padan Aram with his family. After meeting his brother Esau, and determining that all would be well (Genesis 33), Jacob stopped in a place that was later called Shechem. Dinah, the only named daughter of Jacob, who commentators have argued, was about fifteen, went out to meet the girls of the city. Prince Shechem, the son of Hamor, saw her and fell in love with her. The Bible states:

> And when Shechem the son of Hamor the Hivite, prince of the country, saw her, he took her and lay with her, and violated her.

His soul [a]was strongly attracted to Dinah, the daughter of Jacob, and he loved the young woman and spoke [b]kindly to the young woman. So Shechem spoke to his father Hamor, saying, "Get me this young woman as a wife." (Genesis 34:2-4 NKJV).

Yes, Shechem raped Dinah, and in his position as a prince, sought to possess her and take her home for a wife. He reported to his father, and the father met with Jacob to arrange the dowry price and a wedding. Jacob seemed agreeable to the deal, for he did not want a fight. But when Dinah's brothers came home and heard about the violation of their sister, they did not take it lightly. Simeon and Levi told Hamor's sons that for Shechem to marry their sister, all the men of Shechem would have to be circumcised. The men agreed. However, on the day after the circumcision, when the men were sore and were not able to fight back, Simeon and Levi went into the town, slaughtered all the men and took their wives and children.

The actions of Dinah's brothers have raised the following questions about the incident:

1. How should Jacob have reacted to the rape of his only daughter? Should he have quarreled with Dinah or Hamor? Should he have plotted revenge?

2. Did the brothers react correctly? Should they have retaliated in the violent way they did?

3. Should Dinah be blamed for going out to play or party with the girls of the town?

4. Should Dinah take some responsibility for venturing out without knowing the place? We do not know how late it was.

5. Should we excuse her? Some persons have done that, claiming that she was only fifteen years old.

Whatever the response to the questions, the fact remains that rape is awful, it is abuse. It is power and control. Those who study the effects of rape say that rape victims suffer in many ways. Physically, rape victims suffer the gynecological problems that are associated. There is also the possibility of an unwanted pregnancy. There is the likelihood of contracting Sexually Transmissible Diseases (STDs). Psychologically, rape victims suffer immediate conditions such as anxiety, Post-Traumatic Stress Disorder (PTSD), depression, self-blame, shame, confusion, even leading to suicide. Socially, there is "secondary victimization," such as being called names, unworthy to be put in this reflection. There is also isolation, victim-blaming and shaming, and other forms of stigmatization.

This reflection is intended to focus our attention on the tragedy of rape. The intent is for us to ask ourselves, How effective are we in responding to rape victims and their cry for healing? Do we help them to heal or are we continuing to hurt them?

Reflecting on the discussion

1. What new insights that you have gained from the discussion?

2. Are there experiences that you encountered that could have been disastrous but for the grace of God?

3. Write a blessing that you desire for today, and for which you need to pray.

THE DEATH OF A CAREGIVER

Now Deborah, Rebekah's nurse, died, and she was buried below Bethel under the terebinth tree. So the name of it was called [a]Allon Bachuth.

– **Genesis 35:8 NKJV**

THE DEATH OF A CAREGIVER

Have you ever met any of them? Especially women who have given up their entire life to care for others? I can think of some women who have even gone to live with a family while putting on hold other interests in their lives. Some of them might be related to the family, but there are the charitable ones who seem like they are born to care. They work from behind the scenes, just caring for others.

I know of one young woman I will call Martha (not her real name) who lived with a friend of our family. She moved in as a family helper to take care of a newborn son. Within a few years, the father and mother divorced, but she stayed to give support to the mother, I will name Joanna, and the son for a long time. A deep bond developed between Joanna and Martha, and both became inseparable sisters. One day I saw Martha, and in speaking with her, she said, "only death could separate us because I would hate to see Ms. Joanna suffer again the way she suffered when Mr. Don (alias)left her." Death did finally separate them, as the stress of the brokenness made Joanna sick, to the point of being almost nonfunctional. Finally, she succumbed to the ravages of illness. Since the death of Joanna, I have been wondering what has happened to Martha. I know she is alive but didn't know where to find her. On returning to an event in that country, my wife saw her but was unable to get to her. She slipped away in the crowd. O how I wished I could have spoken with her. I cannot help but think of how she gave her entire life to support

Joanna to the very end. Martha is one of many others I know, who have given their lives as caregivers.

In Genesis 35:8, we read about an obscure caregiver named Deborah. As is told, "Now Deborah, Rebekah's nurse died, and she was buried below Bethel under the terebinth tree. So, the name of it was called Allon Bachuth." This is the second time we hear about the nurse of Rebekah. In the first instance, she was only mentioned as Rebekah's nurse when she accompanied her on the journey to the Land of Canaan, where Rebekah was to meet Isaac. All it says is, "So they sent off their sister Rebekah and her nurse" (Gen. 24:59). The next time we hear of her is on the occasion of her death. The mention of Deborah's death is of interest because Rebekah's death is not mentioned in the Bible.

The point I am making is that there is a place for the obscure. Some people who do not seem to have had a prominent place in life became known at death when their contribution to the world came to light. We do not know anything else about Deborah except that she was "Rebekah's nurse." But the fact that she lived with the family as long as she did, some scholars argue that Deborah might have been about 150 years or more when she died, speaks volumes about her character. The fact that the Bible took note that she was buried in a special place that Jacob called Allon Bachuth, in Hebrew "the place of weeping," tells of the impact that she must have had on the life of the family. Although Rebekah was the mother of Jacob and Esau, one should not discount the care of the nanny, Deborah. She had a motherly instinct. Of all the servants that Rebekah took with her, Deborah is the only one to be mentioned by name, and that suggests that she was a special woman in the family. Although there is no record of her deeds, it is not far-fetched to say that Rebekah appreciated Deborah's support as they worked as a team to keep Esau from killing Jacob. And Rebekah must have been glad to have a second pair of watchful eyes to supervise two robust, growing boys as she got some needed rest. Deborah was probably an excellent caregiver for both that Jacob and Esau were present at her funeral, without expressing any resentment. Their attitude demonstrates the love and respect they had for Deborah.

As has been noted, Deborah must have been kind, courageous, confident, strong, loving, and caring. She must have been a great counselor and advisor to Rebekah, and one who had the respect of all around the home. Surely, all in the family must have loved her.

Shakespeare puts it in the mouth of Mark Anthony, at the burial of Julius Caesar, to say, **"The evil that men do lives after them; the good is oft interred with their bones."** Such might be the way that human beings think of many lives. Their good deeds are forgotten, while the evil is remembered. Of course, at funerals and memorial services, some individuals make an effort to create a perfect dead. I have often thought that if it were possible to awaken from the coffin, the dead would get up and wonder, "Is it I"? Who are they talking about? Yes, human beings might falsify a character. They might fail to have clarity on the truth of one's life. They might seek to exaggerate even the good. But thankfully, God knows the truth about each of us.

Deborah lived a long life. She died and was buried under an oak tree. She did not get interned with the patriarchs or matriarchs, but heaven took note of her place of burial, in so much that she is among the mentionable of the Bible. Death is life's inevitable. Even if one lives long in this world, one needs to remember what Ralph Waldo Emerson said, "It is not length of life, but depth of life" that truly matters. Deborah mattered, and when she passed, those who mourned her did so with sincerity.

Reflecting on the discussion

1. What new insights that you have gained from the discussion?

2. Has there been any experience you faced that could have turned into defeat, but for the grace of God?

3. Write a blessing that you desire for today, and for which you need to pray.

MARRYING FOR THE RIGHT REASON

⁶ Then Judah took a wife for Er his firstborn, and her name *was* Tamar. ⁷ But Er, Judah's firstborn, was wicked in the sight of the Lord, and the Lord killed him. ⁸ And Judah said to Onan, "Go in to your brother's wife and marry her, and raise up an heir to your brother." ⁹ But Onan knew that the heir would not be his; and it came to pass, when he went in to his brother's wife, that he emitted on the ground, lest he should give an heir to his brother. ¹⁰ And the thing which he did displeased the Lord; therefore He killed him also.

- **Genesis 38:6-10 NKJV**

MARRYING FOR THE RIGHT REASON

Most individuals who think of marrying, want to marry Mr. Right or Mrs. Right. These days when so many marriages are falling apart, many individuals are blaming the fact that they married "the wrong person." The reality is that marriages have been getting messed up for a long time. I could point to some cases much earlier than that of Basemath, but hers is one which I find very interesting. If you have never heard of her, she was the third wife of Esau. Remember Esau, the brother of Jacob, who sold his birthright for a little bowl of soup? He married two Canaanite women - Adah, the daughter of Elon the Hittite, and Aholibamah, the daughter of Anah, daughter of Zibeon the Hivite. The marriages grieved his parents, who felt that these women were idolaters. Esau, seeing that his brother Jacob was blessed and sent away by their parents to find a wife among the family members in Padan Aram, went to his Uncle Ishmael's household and married his **daughter** Basemath, who was his cousin. Some commentators argue that Esau changed Basemath's name to Mahalath (cf. Genesis 28:6-9). We are not told what kind of marriage it turned out to be, but what we are told in Esau's genealogical tree in Genesis 36:1-5 (NKJV) is this:

> Now this *is* the genealogy of Esau, who is Edom. ² Esau took his wives from the daughters of Canaan: Adah the daughter of Elon the Hittite; Aholibamah[a] the daughter of Anah, the daughter of Zibeon the Hivite; ³ and Basemath, Ishmael's daughter, sister of Neba-

joth. ⁴ Now Adah bore Eliphaz to Esau, and Basemath bore Reuel. ⁵ And [b]Aholibamah bore Jeush, Jaalam, and Korah. These *were* the sons of Esau who were born to him in the land of Canaan.

The Bible record quoted below says, that when Jacob returned from Padan Aram, Esau took his wives and moved away from Canaan.

6 Then Esau took his wives, his sons, his daughters, and all the persons of his household, his cattle and all his animals, and all his goods which he had gained in the land of Canaan, and went to a country away from the presence of his brother Jacob. ⁷ For their possessions were too great for them to dwell together, and the land where they were strangers could not support them because of their livestock. ⁸ So Esau dwelt in Mount Seir. Esau *is* Edom. (Genesis 36:6-8 NKJV).

In reflecting on the character of Esau in the book of Hebrews (12:16), translators tell us that Esau was a "vile," or "profane," or "sexually immoral" or "unspiritual" man. This description of the man should give us pause to think of Basemath. Esau was trying to please his parents and married Basemath. We are not privy to Basemath's religious beliefs but it seems that hers were more acceptable to Esau's parents than that of the two wives before her. Basemath was the daughter of Ishmael, the son of Hagar, Abraham's Egyptian wife. Supposing she learned Abraham's way of worship from Ishmael, one might suspect that Esau's "rough" character must have been a burden to Basemath. From my research, Basemath's name means "fragrance" or "sweet smile." Can you imagine the burden of her life living with a man like Esau?

Marriage should be a covenant of blessing. It is not just a Christian thing. It was given to humanity from the Garden of Eden (cf. Genesis 1:26-27), that is, before humanity decided to rebel against God and seek their own way (cf. Genesis 3). It was given for our joy and the protection of the family. We are also told that marriage influences the success or failure of one's life. It impacts the lives of children who are in the covenant circle. And that it has a profound impact on a person's destiny.

Those who understand the significance of the marriage bond know that when they are contemplating marriage, they must think of the character of the one they are marrying. Before marriage, we are told that every woman (and man, alike) should ask, "How will this marriage affect my destiny?"

Yes, I have used Basemath's marriage to Esau in my framework, to speak to anyone who is getting married about the seriousness of the decision they are to make. Should one get married only to please their parents? Should one get married to please oneself? Or should one get married to please God?

Here are some crucial questions one should ask themselves before getting married:

Am I using marriage to enhance my status in life? Am I getting married for economic reasons? (In the USA the question is asked often) Am I getting married to get a visa? Am I getting married to enhance my reputation in a community? Am I getting married because of the fear of staying single? Am I getting married because I will feel more secure – I will sleep better? Am I getting married because of pressure from my friends or parents? Am I getting married because I fear my biological clock for childbearing will run out soon?

Yes, people get married for a host of reasons. Many also seem to forget the main ingredients that make marriages work. Key elements such as love, spirituality, communicability, commitment, covenanting, morality, integrity, decency, dignity, kindness, caring, and all the positive character qualities that make a woman a woman, or a man and a man are often missing, thus the predicament of many lives.

My challenge to you lies in these two questions:

Are you prepared to settle for an Esau?

If you are married, planning to get married or planning to stay single, what is the quality of your character?

Reflecting on the discussion

1. What new insights that you have gained from the discussion?

2. Has there been an experience that you've had that could have turned into defeat, but for the grace of God?

3. Write a blessing that you desire for today, and for which you need to pray.

LIVING IN A CULTURE OF OPPRESSION

Now in the process of time the daughter of Shua, Judah's wife, died; and Judah was comforted and went up to his sheepshearers at Timnah, he and his friend Hirah the Adullamite. ¹³ And it was told Tamar, saying, "Look, your father-in-law is going up to Timnah to shear his sheep." ¹⁴ So she took off her widow's garments, covered *herself* with a veil and wrapped herself, and sat in an open place which *was* on the way to Timnah; for she saw that Shelah was grown, and she was not given to him as a wife. ¹⁵ When Judah saw her, he thought she *was* a harlot, because she had covered her face. ¹⁶ Then he turned to her by the way, and said, "Please let me come in to you"; for he did not know that she *was* his daughter-in-law.

So she said, "What will you give me that you may come in to me?"

¹⁷ And he said, "I will send a young goat from the flock."

So she said, "Will you give *me* a pledge till you send *it?*"

¹⁸ Then he said, "What pledge shall I give you?"

So she said, "Your signet and cord, and your staff that *is* in your hand." Then he gave *them* to her and went in to her, and she conceived by him. ¹⁹ So she arose and went away and laid aside her veil and put on the garments of her widowhood.

²⁰ And Judah sent the young goat by the hand of his friend the Adullamite, to receive *his* pledge from the woman's hand, but he did not find her. ²¹ Then he asked the men of that place, saying, "Where is the harlot who *was* [b]openly by the roadside?"

And they said, "There was no harlot in this *place*."

²² So he returned to Judah and said, "I cannot find her. Also, the men of the place said there was no harlot in this *place*."

²³ Then Judah said, "Let her take *them* for herself, lest we be shamed; for I sent this young goat and you have not found her." **– Genesis 38:12-23 NKJV**

LIVING IN A CULTURE OF OPPRESSION

It has been a common phenomenon throughout history, in various societies of the world, that women have faced oppression. It is a fact that in the many societies and cultural communities, women could not own property, inherit land and wealth, participate in religious leadership or share equal political rights with men. Even in societies where women obtained some such rights, women complain of receiving less pay than men, of being raped and sexually harassed, or facing other actions that suggest that they are still feeling oppressed.

In facing the conditions of oppression, many women are ambivalent as to how they might respond to the pressures coming from their government, their church, or their family. How does a woman react to a system of justice that does not give her an equal shot at life? Is she expected to "humble" herself, claiming that it is her calling to suffer, in quietness?

I do not wish to tell every woman how to respond. However, I have often mused at how one disreputable biblical character responded. Her story is full of intrigue. In Genesis 38, Tamar got married to two of the sons of Judah. Er, Judah's first son, Tamar's first husband, died before they had a child. According to the cultural tradition Onan, the second son, was forced to marry Tamar. He was not happy for the marriage, mainly because any son born to the union was named for Er, the older brother, and the first husband of Tamar. To avoid pregnancy, Onan "spilled his sperm," that is, *coitus interruptus*. The scriptural comment is that he received divine condemnation and died early. According to the tradition, Judah should have given his third son Shelah to Tamar as a husband. Judah was fearful that Shelah would have died like his other sons, so he suggested that Tamar wait until Shelah got older. After Shelah grew up and Tamar noticed that Judah did not fulfill his promise of giving the third son for her husband, she felt she had to find a way to bring an heir to Judah's lineage.

Upon hearing that Judah's wife died, Tamar devised a plan. At the end of the time of mourning, Judah planned a trip to Timnath to shear his sheep. Tamar, knowing that it was sheep-shearing time, Upon disguised herself as a prostitute and sat at the apex of the road that led to Judah's destination. As Judah was passing, he saw a woman dressed under a veil, as prostitutes did, and he requested her services. Tamar's ruse worked. She made a bargain with Judah for a goat. However, since he did not have the goat present with him, she asked for security. He gave his staff, seal, and cord. When Judah reached his destination, he sent the goat to Timnath, to the supposed prostitute, and in turn, collect his staff, seal, and cord. The messenger could not find the woman, and when he asked about her, the villagers told that they did not know of any prostitute in the area (Genesis 38:12-23). When Judah found out that there was no such woman in the area, he was confused.

Three months after his encounter with the woman in Timnath, Judah found out that his daughter-in-law was pregnant. In judging the case,

Judah rendered his decision that Tamar should be burnt to death according to the law. This verdict from Judah caused Tamar to reveal herself. She showed the three pledges and declared that she was pregnant for the owner of the items she showed. Judah was forced to confess his relationship with Tamar publicly. From the encounter, a set of twins called Zerah and Perez were born. Who would think that Perez would become the great grandfather of David (cf. Ruth 4:18-22). Later Perez and Tamar were named among the progenitors of Jesus Christ (cf. Matthew 1:3).

Yes, here is a most convoluted story. It reflects how oppression might cause a person to act. Do we need to use it as a way to tell women how to respond to family dysfunction? One of the things that we learn is that Tamar was not willing to sit around and allow herself to cry for the rest of her life. I might not have responded as Tamar did. You might not react in that way either. However, in Tamar's culture, women were treated as valuable only if they could bring forth a child of inheritance. Tamar used what she thought best, disguise, manipulation, and seduction by pretending to be a prostitute, to gain status as a woman of value. One might say she was wrong. Others might excuse her by saying that is what oppression does to women by allowing them to use undignified means to find the path of liberation.

But what is clear is that from this story, is that although Tamar might have used an untimely response, God was watching and covered her disgrace with grace. We know that in the struggle for respect and equality, women make many mistakes. But any woman who is willing to confess and repent, God is faithful and ready to bring a blessing out of the errors. God knows the circumstances of every life and can use the most complicated situation to bring forth a blessing.

In various circumstances, we might have used unethical means to reach our ends and to receive the favor of God. However, let us not forget that God does not forsake us. The prophet Isaiah reminds us of God's love by stating, "If you are willing and obedient, you will eat the good things of the land; but if you resist and rebel, you will be devoured by the sword." For the mouth of the Lord has spoken." (Isaiah 1:19, 20 NIV). Yes, indeed, God does not commend any form of manipulation or deception, but he sees us in our circumstances of oppression and hears our cry for justice. One of my seminary professors, Dr. James Cone, titled one of his books, God of the Oppressed. And for me, this is a profound characterization of God. God is still superintending our situation.

Reflecting on the discussion

1. What new insights that you have gained from the discussion?

2. Have you had any experience lately that could have turned into defeat, but for the grace of God?

3. Write a blessing that you desire for today, and for which you need to pray.

SHE SAID HE DID IT

¹¹ But it happened about this time, when Joseph went into the house to do his work, and none of the men of the house *was* inside, ¹² that she caught him by his garment, saying, "Lie with me." But he left his garment in her hand, and fled and ran outside. ¹³ And so it was, when she saw that he had left his garment in her hand and fled outside, ¹⁴ that she called to the men of her house and spoke to them, saying, "See, he has brought in to us a Hebrew to [f]mock us. He came in to me to lie with me, and I cried out with a loud voice. ¹⁵ And it happened, when he heard that I lifted my voice and cried out, that he left his garment with me, and fled and went outside."

¹⁶ So she kept his garment with her until his master came home. ¹⁷ Then she spoke to him with words like these, saying, "The Hebrew servant whom you brought to us came in to me to mock me; ¹⁸ so it happened, as I lifted my voice and cried out, that he left his garment with me and fled outside."

¹⁹ So it was, when his master heard the words which his wife spoke to him, saying, "Your servant did to me after this manner," that his anger was aroused

Genesis 39:11-19 NKJV

SHE SAID HE DID IT

At a time when the "Me Too" movement has been so vocal concerning the sexual harassment and assault of men toward women, it is challenging for men to call out the indiscretions of women toward men. However, for anyone willing to listen to the whispers, it should be understood that not only are men seducers of women, but women are seducers of men. The Collins English Dictionary, notes that "A seducer is someone, usually a man, who seduces someone else." Or "a person or thing that seduces; esp., a man who seduces a woman sexually." The example sentence in the Dictionary states, "Was the anonymous father conceivably the same man, a seducer of young women whose very namelessness left endless room for speculation," makes for an exciting discussion. But what is most striking in the sentence is that the focus is on "men" as seducers. But, as has been noted, historically, women have also been found to be seducers also.

The ancient story of Mrs. Potipher is rather intriguing because it provides a clue in the way one woman sought to seduce a man. Do you remember it? Joseph's brothers sold him into slavery and taken to Egypt by the Ishmaelites, where Potiphar, a master in Egyptian political life, bought him. The Biblical telling is quite descriptive, and one needs not place a brush upon it. It says in Genesis 39:3-21 NIV:

> When his (Joseph's) master saw that the LORD was with him and that the LORD gave him success in everything he did, Joseph found

favor in his eyes and became his attendant. Potiphar put Joseph in charge of his household, and he entrusted to his care everything he owned. From the time he put him in charge of his household and of all that he owned, the LORD blessed the household of the Egyptian because of Joseph. The blessing of the LORD was on everything Potiphar had, both in the house and in the field. So he left in Joseph's care everything he had; with Joseph in charge, he did not concern himself with anything except the food he ate. Now Joseph was well-built and handsome, and after a while, his master's wife took notice of Joseph and said, "Come to bed with me!" But he refused. "With me in charge," he told her, "my master does not concern himself with anything in the house; everything he owns he has entrusted to my care. No one is greater in this house than I am. My master has withheld nothing from me except you because you are his wife. How then could I do such a wicked thing and sin against God?" And though she spoke to Joseph day after day, he refused to go to bed with her or even be with her. One day he went into the house to attend to his duties, and none of the household servants was inside. She caught him by his cloak and said, "Come to bed with me!" But he left his cloak in her hand and ran out of the house. When she saw that he had left his cloak in her hand and had run out of the house, she called her household servants. "Look," she said to them, "this Hebrew has been brought to us to make sport of us! He came in here to sleep with me, but I screamed. When he heard me scream for help, he left his cloak beside me and ran out of the house." She kept his cloak beside her until his master came home. Then she told him this story: "That Hebrew slave you brought us came to me to make sport of me. But as soon as I screamed for help, he left his cloak beside me and ran out of the house." When his master heard the story his wife told him, saying, "This is how your slave treated me," he burned with anger. Joseph's master took him and put him in prison, the place where the king's prisoners were confined. But while Joseph was there in prison, the LORD was with him; he showed him kindness and granted him favor in the eyes of the prison warden.

Commentators have suggested that the young man Joseph was a real specimen of a man. He was strong, confident, courageous, dignified, disciplined, talented, skilled, wise, and spiritual. He could stand out in any crowd. These qualities drew the attention of Mrs. Potipher. As Joseph moved about her house, day after day, she kept her eyes on him until one day, when the opportunity came, and she tried to seduce him. We may never know her words, but one might imagine her saying the following words quoted in the book of Proverbs, which might have been that might have been collected from Egypt:

> My husband is not at home; he has gone on a long journey. [20] He took his purse filled with money and will not be home till full moon." [21] With persuasive words, she [tried to lead] him astray; she [tried to] seduce him with her smooth talk. (Proverbs 7:19-21 NIV).

As Joseph fled from Mrs. Potiphar, she grabbed at his clothes, and he left his outer garment or part of it, in her hands. When her husband came home, she showed the garment and recited her version of the story to him. Her husband put Joseph in jail. Many commentators insist that Potiphar did what was most favorable to do, but he did not believe his wife.

This story begs the question, Can we believe all the stories of men who claim that "it was the woman who seduced them? " Should we believe those of the women who claim that "it was the man who seduced or sexually harassed them?

While we might not be able to answer each question in any systematic way, what we know is that there are women who seduce men, by their words, dress or actions, as well as men who seduce women. And some women lie concerning seduction, as well as men.

What we should understand in all the charges and counter-charges is that each woman or man needs to have personal integrity. If I were placed in jail with a false accusation of sexual indiscretion, do I know the truth concerning the innocence of my life? Does God know the truth about me? Am I able to stand before the throne of God as a guiltless person? And, yes, it is true, that while I might be able to get away from jail here on earth, it is a fact that "we must all appear before the judgment seat of Christ, so that each of us may receive what is due us for the things done while in the body, whether good or bad." (1 Corinthians 5:10).

Reflecting on the discussion

1. What new insights that you have gained from the discussion?

2. Has there been an experience you had that could have turned into defeat, but for the grace of God?

3. Write a blessing that you desire for today, and for which you need to pray.

WHEN A MIXED MARRIAGE BECOMES A BLESSING

And Pharaoh called Joseph's name Zaphnath-paaneah, and he gave him to wife **Asenath**, the daughter of **Potipherah** priest of **On**. And Joseph went out over all the land of Egypt. - **Genesis 41:45**

And unto Joseph were born two sons before the years of famine came, which Asenath, the daughter of Potipherah priest of On bare unto him. - **Genesis 41:50**

And unto Joseph in the land of Egypt were born Manasseh and Ephraim, which Asenath the daughter of Potipherah priest of On bare unto him. - **Genesis 46:20**

WHEN A MIXED MARRIAGE BECOMES A BLESSING

When Megan Markle married Prince Harry, some individuals argued that even though she was famous, had some money, and was a successful Hollywood star, **she had married up.** She became royalty.

I do not know what might be said about Asenath, the wife of Joseph. She was likely aware that Joseph had just been taken out of Pharaoh's jail. Joseph had interpreted Pharaoh's dreams and was about to be promoted to be the second ruler in the kingdom of Egypt. What many might have said of her is that **she married down** because she married a "jailbird." Asenath was the daughter of the high priest of On. The high priesthood of On was held in high esteem because On was the center for the worshipers of the sun god. On, which also went by the name of Heliopolis, was called "the city of the sun." The priests of On were thought to be very powerful and wise. Since Joseph was now considered a wise man, Pharaoh took him, changed his name to Zaphnath- Paaneah, and gave him Asenath as a wife (Genesis 41:45).

We might not know everything that was going through Pharaoh's mind as he gave Asenath to Joseph to be his wife. But it is significant because Pharoah might have thought of it as part of his endorsement of Joseph to the high status to which he would put him as governor of Egypt. We do not know what else Asenath did for Joseph, except that she bore him two sons, Manasseh and Ephraim, who would come to prominence as tribal heads in Israel.

Those who might wonder about the impact of Asenath's religion on Joseph and their two sons might suggest that Asenath likely changed her faith. Beyond that, we might settle it that God used the situation for a mighty purpose because, as Manasseh and Ephraim became tribal heads, the tribe of Levi was released to become priests and temple servants for the Israelites. In effect, God made this mixed marriage a blessing. The Apostle Paul contends that if a Christian is married to an unbeliever, the believer needs not run away, for the unbeliever might be brought into a life of holiness by the believer. He also suggests that the believer should not rush for a separation or divorce, using the pretext of his or her faith. Such separation or divorce should only come if the unbeliever seeks to walk away (1 Corinthians 7:10-14). The question of mixed marriage can be very complicated and should be avoided. However, if one is in it, one needs to seek divine aid to resolve the issues connected with it.

Now, what strikes me most about Asenath is not spoken of in the texts about her marriage and the bearing of the two sons. But I contend that it must have been interesting to live with a man whose brothers sold him into slavery. Did she have any feelings of resentment toward the brothers? Did she say, "All things work together for good to them that love the Lord, to them who are the called according to his purpose" (Romans 8:28)? I do not know that she knew this text or held to such a concept. How did she react when the brothers of Joseph came to Egypt, and Joseph told her of their visit and later welcome them? Even though

Asenath's name is not mentioned again, yet I imagine that she must have had the same spirit of forgiveness as her husband, Joseph. Asenath must have reconciled the issue to welcome Joseph's family and then to send her children to spend time around the brothers and their families.

Forgiveness, as we might know, is among the greatest gifts that God has given to humanity. This is why it is said:

> Without forgiveness, there is no future meaning in our lives.
> Without forgiveness, there is no remission of sin.
> Without forgiveness, there is no redemption.
> Without forgiveness, there is no love.
> Without forgiveness, there is no reconciliation.
> Without forgiveness, there is no peace.
> Without forgiveness, there is no joy.

We must credit Joseph with the blessed life that his father and siblings enjoyed in Egypt; but, also credit Asenath. We assume that from behind the scene, and undoubtedly beside Joseph, she must have used skills as the daughter of the high priest of On to build a relationship with her in-laws. Of course, we need not only think of her power and popularity as the means of her influence, but of her forgiving spirit. By forgiving the brothers as her husband, Joseph did, Asenath helped him to avoid a daily round of life without complaint or criticism. She made Joseph's spirit free so that he could be among the most effective governors that Egypt has ever seen.

As you think of Asenath, ask yourself, How can I shed a positive influence to make the world a better place?

Reflecting on the discussion

1. What new insights that you have gained from the discussion?

2. Are there experiences you faced that could have turned into defeat, but by the grace of God, turned out right?

3. Write a blessing that you desire for today, and for which you need to pray.

THE RESISTERS

Then the king of Egypt spoke to the Hebrew midwives, of whom the name of one *was* Shiphrah and the name of the other Puah; [16] and he said, "When you do the duties of a midwife for the Hebrew women and see *them* on the birth stools, if it *is* a son, then you shall kill him; but if it *is* a daughter, then she shall live." [17] But the midwives feared God, and did not do as the king of Egypt commanded them, but saved the male children alive. [18] So the king of Egypt called for the midwives and said to them, "Why have you done this thing, and saved the male children alive?"

[19] And the midwives said to Pharaoh, "Because the Hebrew women *are* not like the Egyptian women; for they *are* lively and give birth before the midwives come to them."

[20] Therefore God dealt well with the midwives, and the people multiplied and grew very mighty. [21] And so it was, because the midwives feared God, that He provided households for them.

- Exodus 1:15-21 NKJV

THE RESISTERS

Women are fighting back. This is what the Me Too Movement, Mothers Against Drunk Driving (MAD), National Advocates for Pregnant Women (NAPW), Mom's Demand Action (MDA), and other such movements are doing to resist the evils that societies have sought to use to destroy women and their children. While I highly regard these movements, it is not my interest here to affirm or disaffirm them, but I take note that it is a fact that in the history of social resistance that women have played a significant role.

Among the greatest of resisters that I know are two obscure women in the Bible. They were not part of any significant movement. They did their jobs so unobtrusively that it mystified Pharaoh. Hear their story as it is written in Exodus 1:15-21:

> Then the king of Egypt spoke to the Hebrew midwives, of whom the name of one *was* Shiphrah and the name of the other Puah; [16] and he said, "When you do the duties of a midwife for the Hebrew women and see *them* on the birth stools, if it *is* a son, then you shall kill him; but if it *is* a daughter, then she shall live." [17] But the midwives feared God, and did not do as the king of Egypt commanded them, but saved the male children alive. [18] So the king of Egypt called for the midwives and said to them, "Why have you done this thing, and saved the male children alive?" [19] And the midwives said to Pharaoh, "Because the Hebrew women *are* not like the Egyptian

women; for they [a]*are* lively and give birth before the midwives come to them." **20** Therefore God dealt well with the midwives, and the people multiplied and [b]grew very mighty. **21** And so it was, because the midwives feared God, that He [c]provided households for them.

Only if you had been paying close attention to Biblical history would you have known the names of Shiphrah and Puah. But as is stated, they were among the greatest of resisters in history. Through their effort, many male babies of Israel were saved, and thus, the Hebrew nation multiplied. They saw the injustice in the law that Pharaoh had issued for the death of every male child born to the Israelites, and they resisted. Their motherly instincts kicked in, and they acted with urgency. They were persistent. They did not vacillate. They did not go around asking friends what the right thing to do was. They understood who was in charge of giving and taking life, and they took their cues from Him. They knew when to speak and when to be silent. They knew how to make the right decisions and act promptly. They were risk-takers and didn't seem to put their lives first. They saw the ills perpetrated against God's chosen ones, and they acted accordingly.

Shiphrah and Puah were god-fearing women who understood what the apostle Peter would later say when he and the apostle John were brought before the Sanhedrin and threatened for preaching the gospel. Peter responded, "We are to serve God rather than human beings" (Acts 5:27-29). In effect, they would not procrastinate. They would not vacillate.

They sensed the need to be decisive, and they took their wisdom from the divine.

They did not go with the crowd. They took, with utter seriousness, their personal responsibilities.

In this context, we might think of what happened in Europe during WWII when the Nazi overran the Netherlands. Corrie Ten Boom, a powerful resister, used her house to save many lives. While the majority of the population were succumbing to the oppressive behavior of the Gestapo's, Corrie Ten Boom resisted Hitler's ideology. Today, Corrie Ten Boom's house is in the movie " The Hiding Place," but amid the distress, it was not a movie. Corrie Ten Boom was willing to sacrifice her very life to save others.

Many questions of interest should come to mind as you reflect on Shiprah and Puah or Corrie Ten Boom and what they were willing to do to resist the abuses perpetrated against children and others. What are you ready to do? What can you do to help with the salvation of the abused children of our day? How much courage do you have to enter into the fray? Have you ever done anything to challenge the conception that abortion is the best road to contraception, for example? How committed are you to the preservation of life? What can you do to save our children?

While I am not asking you to enter into the political conflict on abortion, I am asking you to help those about you to know that there is a better way.

Reflecting on the discussion

1. What new insights that you have gained from the discussion?

2. Has there an experience that you confronted that could have turned into defeat, but for the grace of God?

3. Write a blessing that you desire for today, and for which you need to pray.

THE PROTECTIVE MOTHER

² So the woman conceived and bore a son. And when she saw that he *was* a beautiful *child,* she hid him three months. ³ But when she could no longer hide him, she took an ark of bulrushes for him, daubed it with asphalt and pitch, put the child in it, and laid *it* in the reeds by the river's bank. ⁴ And his sister stood afar off, to know what would be done to him.

— **Exodus 2:2-4 NKJV**

THE PROTECTIVE MOTHER

When my friend Dr. Charles P. Conroy, the executive director of Doctor Franklin Perkins School in Lancaster, Massachusetts, and graduate instructor at Fitchburg (MA) State College, gave me a copy of his epic book, *"Who's Throwing Babies in the River,"* just after its publication in 2001, I never thought that after so many years it would still be so central in my mind. But it still haunts me, even as I see children in cages at our Southern border, as I think of all the children being aborted, abused, and neglected across the land. How deeply are mothers (and fathers) of today engaged in the battle to protect their children? How much thought are we giving to the fact that with all of the throw-away children, we could be losing some of the greatest leaders of all time? These questions demand serious thought.

The thoughts expressed above, project my mind to another time when all boy babies born to Hebrew mothers in Egypt, were ordered to be killed by King Pharaoh. The order led Jochebed, the mother of Moses, to take the greatest risk of her life to save her son. As the story is told in Exodus 2, Jochebed made a basket of bullrushes, daubed it with slime and pitch, put her three-month-old son into it, and laid it on the bank of the crocodile-infested waters of the river Nile. She stationed Miriam, the elder sister of Moses, to watch what would happen to the little basket and the baby inside. It was a bold and daring experiment, but it was successful, for when Pharaoh's daughter came by the river with her maids to bathe, she discovered the basket. She quickly ordered her maids to fetch the basket and notice a baby inside. The princess immediately thought that it must be one of the Hebrew children. Amid the investigation of the contents of the basket, Miriam appeared from her guard post by the side bush. She cleverly offered Pharaoh's daughter a nurse to help with the rearing of the child. Likely, to her surprise, Pharaoh's daughter consented, and Miriam went to get Jochebed, who must have been delighted as she took note of how God was working. Jochebed fulfilled her motherly task of taking care of Moses for twelve years until it was time to hand him over to the queen. She took him to the palace and gave him over to his rescuer. Moses lived there in the palace for the next 28 years.

We do not know how long Jochebed lived after she delivered Moses to the palace. She might have been dead by the time Moses got into trouble for trying to advocate for his people and had to flee Egypt. But we know that when he returned to Egypt from his 40 years in the Midian desert to lead out in the liberation of Israel from Egyptian bondage, Jochebed was not around to greet him. She was the chief architect in his preparation to become one of the greatest leaders of all time. How Jochebed managed to hide her baby in a safe place for the first three months of Moses' life remains a mystery, but her clever design reflects the desperate action of a mother who wanted to save her child. Her ingenious design to preserve the life of her child is noted in the book of Hebrews 11:23 thus, "By faith Moses, when he was born, was hidden three months by his parents because they saw *he was* a beautiful child; and they were not afraid of the king's command." (NKJV).

In reflecting on the protective maternal instinct of Jochebed, I have isolated the following eight points about her.

1. She was a woman of purpose – She determined in her mind that against all the odds, she was going to save her son.

2. She was a woman of faith – Her faith was deeply grounded in God. She handed over everything into God's providential care.

3. She was a woman who dared – Just imagine the risk to her child as he was found, the threat to her life if she were caught, and the risk of placing her child on the crocodile-infested water. She knew that it was what she had to do if she were going to save her child.

4. She was a woman of discernment – Wisdom beyond the ordinary. It must have been rooted in the divine. Her clever design to spare the life of her child is not within the grasp of ordinary human beings.

5. She was a woman of profound discipline – She understood how to control herself as she appeared before Pharaoh's daughter.

6. She was a woman of dedication – She set her goal for what she wanted to do and followed it to the end. In protecting and training her child, she knew she had to seat the Hebrew values deeply. And such is evident because even though he went to the palace at age 12, he never forgot the education that she instilled in him.

7. She was a woman of decision. She was quick in thinking and decisive in following through. She did not waiver on what she had to do.

8. She was a prayerful woman – While she waited to see what would happen to her son- both on the banks of the River Nile and at the Palace, without a doubt, she must have been praying for divine protection.

For all we know, Jochebed's life was exemplary - she gave her all for her child. Those who have sought the meaning of her name state that it means "Jehovah is her glory." I believe that not every mother will have a name that might have the same meaning as Jochebed's, but all can be dedicated to God. They can, by their commitment and dedication, offer the same kind of care, training, and protection to their children. By doing so, they will receive the commendation of the divine - "'Well *done*, good and faithful servant; you were faithful over a few things, I will make you ruler over many things. Enter into the joy of your lord.'" (Matthew 25:21, 23).

Reflecting on the discussion

1. What new insights that you have gained from the discussion?

2. Has there been any experience you faced that could have turned into defeat, but for the grace of God?

3. Write a blessing that you desire for today, and for which you need to pray.

A CARING SISTER

Then his sister said to Pharaoh's daughter, "Shall I go and call a nurse for you from the Hebrew women, that she may nurse the child for you?"

-Exodus 2:2 NKJV

A CARING SISTER

Among our seven grandchildren are two sisters, one sister with two brothers, and two brothers. What is most admirable about these three sets of grandchildren is how the older ones protect the younger ones. One might argue that it is instinctive that older siblings will protect younger ones, but I have seen otherwise. Although some sisters and brothers might spend their time fighting later in life, the instinct is to protect each other as in the earlier part of their lives.

The above brings me to the story of Miriam, the sister of Moses. Do you remember her? In Exodus chapter 2, she is introduced to readers by the River Nile watching the basket her mother placed there with her baby brother Moses hidden in it. Pharaoh, king of Egypt, ordered the destruction of all Hebrew boy babies, so Moses' mother, Jochebed, along with his sister Miriam, devised a plan to save the baby by placing him on the river in a basket daubed with pitch. Jochebed told Miriam to hide in the bushes by the river to watch what would happen. We are not sure how long Miriam was watching, but while she was keeping guard, Pharaoh's daughter came down to the river with her maids to bathe. She saw the basket with the baby and pitied him. Miriam arose from her hiding place and asked the princess if she wanted a Hebrew woman to nurse the baby for her. The princess agreed, and Miriam went quickly to call her mother. The princess arranged with Jochebed to nurse the baby with the instruction that she should bring him back to her when he was older. Miriam's prompt action helped to save the infant Moses.

When Moses was eighty years old and was called to lead the Hebrew slaves out of Egypt, once again, Miriam enters the picture along with her brother Aaron as Moses' helpers. Aside from being a caregiver and helper, Miriam was a gifted poet and musician, so when the Hebrews crossed the Red Sea and were free from their Egyptian masters, she led out in the victory song, with timbrel and dance. (cf. Exodus 15). Note some of the powerful words, "Sing to the Lord, for he is highly exalted. Both horse and driver he has hurled into the sea." It is here that Miriam is called a "prophetess."

After Miriam did so much to support her brother Moses, it is tragic that she would be jealous of him. Numbers 12 states how Miriam and her brother Aaron began to grumble. Both of them criticized Moses for marrying a Cushite or Ethiopian woman, and for excluding them from participating in the selection of the seventy elders. Hear their words of complaint, "Has the Lord spoken only through Moses?' they asked. 'Hasn't he also spoken through us?" (Numbers 12:2). The complaint led to the judgment of God against them. Miriam became a leper and was removed from the camp for seven days. Moses prayed for them, and God brought Miriam healing.

The story is of profound interest because it leads me to think that even with the best protective instinct that a sister (or a brother) might have for each other, the devil always seeks to wake up that other instinct-selfishness, that is native to human beings. Call it "sibling jealousy" if you will, or call it resentment, jealousy, or the desire to control, it is all the same spirit that the devil uses to break our relationships with each other, whether in a family or outside of it. You can also call it racism, which is part of the same when we look down on others because of their race, ethnicity, or culture. In essence, we are following the path of the devil, whatever we choose to call it.

Yes, the beautiful picture that I have painted concerning our grandchildren in the first part of the reflection is only part of a story. We have seen them get jealous or angry with each other, not in the way that Miriam got jealous of Moses, yet it is possible to have a fallout.

Just think of it? If one recounted the great qualities of Miriam, one would have to say, she was caring, kind, faithful, perceptive, patient, pious, and poetic. But on a negative note, she was jealous, controlling, disloyal, prideful, and prejudiced.

What is the message to us from Miriam's story? "Therefore, let anyone who thinks that he stands, take heed lest he falls." (1 Corinthians 10:12 ESV). All of us need to watch ourselves for those negatives in our hearts that will destroy our positive tendencies and contributions to life. We need to be especially careful with our propensities to pride and jealousy, for they seem to plague the best of us. We might occupy high positions of trust, but we are not insulated from tendencies to negative behavior. Miriam was in her late eighties or early nineties, and the spirit of evil was still hanging on to her.

I invite you to pray this prayer with me:
May God be merciful to all of us.
Cleanse our hearts from jealousy.
Take away anything that would seek to destroy us.
Protect us from all evil thoughts and actions towards others.
Amen.

Reflecting on the discussion

1. What new insights that you have gained from the discussion?

2. Are there experiences you faced that could have turned into defeat, but, for the grace of God you became an overcomer?

3. Write a blessing that you desire for today, and for which you need to pray.

THE ADOPTIVE MOTHER

And Pharaoh's daughter said to her, "Go." So the maiden went and called the child's mother. ⁹ Then Pharaoh's daughter said to her, "Take this child away and nurse him for me, and I will give *you* your wages." So the woman took the child and nursed him. ¹⁰ And the child grew, and she brought him to Pharaoh's daughter, and he became her son. So she called his name [a]Moses, saying, "Because I drew him out of the water."

– **Exodus 2:8-10 NKJV**

THE ADOPTIVE MOTHER

I do not know your thoughts about the inhumane treatment of children at the Southern border of the United States, but the abuse they are suffering is of grave concern. They are separated from their parents, put into cages, and detained for more extended periods than any humanitarian law allows. I know many people are incensed by what they see and wish that the leaders at the highest level would be sensitive to the outcry against the destruction of children. The President of the United States might not have the will to do so, but someone, such as his daughter, should step in. There must be someone whose conscience can come to life so that God can use him/her to intervene and save the children from the moment of terror. Who that person is, I do not know, but I am praying that someone like Pharaoh's daughter, will emerge to do the right thing, even against the President's desire.

Pharaoh's daughter, referenced in secular history, was one of the most influential women in Egyptian history. Genesis 2:1-8 and Acts 7:20-22, tell how she went against Pharaoh's orders and saved a young Hebrew baby boy who would later become the liberator of the Hebrews. The boy was among the babies that Pharaoh had ordered the midwives to murder. But Pharaoh's daughter helped to save his life. The Bible does not give a name for Pharaoh's daughter. She is called "Pharaoh's daughter." However, secular writers identify her as Queen Hatshepsut, who became one of the most powerful women in Egyptian history.

Hatshepsut went to the river Nile to have a bath. There she discovered the Hebrew baby hidden in a basket by the river. Hatshepsut immediately fell in love with him and took him in her arms. The baby's sister Miriam, who was watching the basket from the bush by the side of the river, came from hiding and inquired if she needed a nurse for the baby. Miriam called her mother, and when she came, Hatshepsut handed the baby over to the mother to be his nurse. The baby remained with his mother until he was grown up to the age of twelve.

Why Hatshepsut did not immediately bring the baby into the palace, we might never be sure. But we can imagine that she was keeping him away from her father, who had issued the death decree for all Hebrew boy babies. The Hebrew people were getting so numerous in the land, that Pharaoh looked for ways to control their rapid growth. Some commentators argue that Hatshepsut knew she was her father's favorite child. However, she could not rely on him, because in his bitterness, he might have killed her. By not taking the child to the palace, she was preserving her father from further despotic actions.

It is said, based on the year that Moses was born, c.1526, Hatshepsut was the only surviving child of Thutmose I, her other two brothers had died. Upon her father's death, c. 1512, she began a 22-year reign as Pharaoh. During her formative years, she watched the Egyptian dynasty ruled by her father, become weaker and weaker. Her father's goal was primarily to conquer other nations while putting the country's infrastructure on the backburner. He stretched his country's military and financial resources to the brink of ruin, thus allowing Egypt to become economically vulnerable to other nations. Although Egypt maintained a reputation as a powerhouse in education, architecture, philosophy, military might, and engineering, it was morally, socially, and spiritually weakened. This weakness Pharaoh blamed on the Hebrews.

Hatshepsut watched the ruthlessness of her father in response to governing the growing minority of the Hebrews. She realized that her father was "grasping at straws" to retain his diminishing power and did so by wiping out vulnerable, defenseless, innocent children. Whether she understood it or not, she became an instrument of salvation for the Hebrew children. Just like Joseph, who came into the palace at an opportune time to bring salvation to his family and the Egyptian nation, so God would use Hatshepsut to prepare the way for the liberation of the Hebrew slaves. We do not know precisely how the Hebrews feared during her reign, but quite likely, she made their condition better than it was during her father's reign.

What can be said of Queen Hatshepsut is that she demonstrated wisdom, courage, and determination to save the boy she found in the river. Her remarkable behavior explains why later generations of Hebrews designated her as a "righteous Gentile." She assisted them in a significant way, even though they thought of her as a nonbeliever.

In our evil time, when the lives of so many children are being destroyed, I wish we had more Hatshepsut's in positions of power to save our children. We cannot allow our fears to drive us to do nothing. We cannot let complacency paralyze us. We need to take some action to bring about the salvation of the future generation. We might never know whether we are saving a leader who will liberate us, but we need to do what we need to do to save some life. We need to pray that God will raise up someone in a position of trust to aide our effort.

Hatshepsut might not be in our midst today, but the same God who allowed her to act in the salvation of Moses is alive today. He can bring someone from the shadows of the palace to the rescue. Pray for it, please.

Reflecting on the discussion:

1. What new insights that you have gained from the discussion?

2. Are there experiences you faced that could have turned into defeat, but for the grace of God?

3. Write a blessing that you desire for today, and for which you need to pray.

HELPERS BECOME SILENT RESISTERS

⁵ Then the daughter of Pharaoh came down to bathe at the river. And her maidens walked along the riverside, and when she saw the ark among the reeds, she sent her maid to get it. ⁶ And when she opened *it*, she saw the child, and behold, the baby wept. So she had compassion on him, and said, "This is one of the Hebrews' children."

- **Exodus 2:5, 6 NKJV**

HELPERS BECOME SILENT RESISTERS

Some time ago, as my wife was reflecting on the story of Moses, she asked, "If the helpers of Queen Hatshepsut had not kept their mouths shut, what would have happened to her and the child she had rescued from the River Nile?" "Talk about Moses," I said, "but think too, that there might have been other baby boys hidden from the onslaught of Pharaoh's orders or decree." Suppose the servants of Hatshepsut were gossipers, or snitches, such as can be found in many communities of the oppressed, the information about the Hebrew baby rescued from the water would have spread "like a palace fire." Moses would have been killed, and as I said, other boys, as well. But in offering their assistance, with resistance, the helpers kept silent. We should not forget that in Nazi Germany, it was needful to understand when to speak out and when to remain silent. Because the young pastor, Dietrich Bonhoeffer spoke out in resistance against Hitler, he lost his life. On the other hand, it was necessary that those, like Corrie Ten Boom, who used their houses as hiding places for Jews and Christian resisters, had learned the power of silent resistance.

Solomon said this, [There is] "a time to keep silence, and a time to speak" (Ecclesiastes 3:7). I do not know the particular reason for him saying what he said. Perhaps he was thinking of utterances such as, "A time to love, and a time to hate; a time of war, and a time of peace." Which is to say, there is a very thin line when one needs to create a balance between venting one's anger and keeping silent. Thomas Carlysle echoes this admonition when he says, "Speech is silver, silence is golden." It is also true that to remain quiet when there is injustice in the land is to be complicit in the injustice. Or as Martin Luther King Jr. said, "There comes a time when **silence is** betrayal." Or, "Our lives begin to end, the day we become silent."

Martin Luther King Jr. taught the art of silent resistance. He encouraged silent prayer in the face of struggle. The truth is that sometimes we talk too much and give the enemy all the ammunition to destroy us. The enemy can know what we are thinking or planning to do and war against us. When he knows everything about us, he can set up a battle plan. Or to point the fingers at our human enemies, too often we allow them in the most secret chambers of our lives. Hence the warning, if you are married, do not share the most intimate secrets of your spousal relationships, not even with a friend. Do not share your marital struggles with others. Do not speak of things you are not sure about. And even when you are confident, there might be times to be silent. One of the great Proverbs says, "he one who has knowledge uses words with restraint, and whoever has understanding is even-tempered. Even fools are thought wise if they keep silent, and discerning if they hold their tongues." (Proverbs 7:26, 27 NIV) Abraham Lincoln is credited with saying, "Better to remain silent and be thought a fool than to speak out and remove all doubt."

The author, Amy Dickerson, says, "Saying nothing sometimes says the most." Jesus told his disciples and some of those he healed, not to tell anyone - keep silent (cf. Mark 7:36; Matthew 8:4; Luke 5:14-16). Jesus wanted them to be silent until they understood what he had done to them. He needed the silence at times so that those healed would not be abused. He also needed the silence so that he could get away from the places where he performed the miracles. It is of interest that no matter Jesus' request, many who were healed went away telling their story, and jeopardized Jesus' safety. In fact, the enemies never stopped hounding Jesus until they had him arrested, tried, and condemned. At His arrest and trial, one of Jesus' greatest weapons of resistance against his false accusers was "silence." (cf. Matthew 26:63; 27:12, 14; John 14:9, 10; 19:10).

Yes, silence can be a powerful weapon. It is not easily interpreted, but it has its highest value as a justification for resistance. We note that:

1. When you have a secret thought, you need to be careful how you express it, for the enemy is always listening to how he can use it to attack you.

2. When you have a relationship that you wish to keep sacred, know the place of silence.

3. Do not share your intimacies with your best friend outside of the one to whom you are committed.

4. When you do not have knowledge of an issue, it is better to be quiet than to open your mouth and seem like a fool – resist the temptation to jump to conclusions and then express them.

5. If you are angry and feeling outraged, be careful of what you say, when you say what you say, and how you say what you might say.

6. Never forget to be respectful, like Jesus was.

7. If you see the oppression that demands silence, learn how to use silence.

The servants of Queen Hatshepsut were effective because they were silent resisters. Sometimes you might endanger your life by over-speaking. Know when it is needful to use silence, so that you and others might live. When you present your prayers of resistance to God, pray silently. "God understands your heartache; he sees the falling tear."

If you are having difficulty in the use of silent resistance, learn from your children. They know how to use silence as resistance. They know how to bottle up their fears, anxieties, and rage in the face of coercion. They use silence as a means not to cooperate. Their example is not one that an adult might wish to emulate in every way since rebellious actions do imply disrespect. However, we can all learn silence as a means of self-discipline. And when it is most needful, especially as a weapon of resistance, let us use it effectively, as did Hatshepsut helpers.

Reflecting on the discussion

1. What new insights that you have gained from the discussion?

2. Has there been an experience that you faced lately that might have turned into defeat, but, by the grace of God, has turned into a triumph?

3. Write a blessing that you desire for today, and for which you need to pray.

BEYOND INTUITION

And it came to pass on the way, at the encampment, that the Lord met him and sought to kill him. [25] Then Zipporah took a sharp stone and cut off the foreskin of her son and cast *it* at *Moses'* feet, and said, "Surely you *are* a husband of blood to me!" [26] So He let him go. Then she said, "*You are* a husband of blood!"—because of the circumcision.

- Exodus 4:24-26

BEYOND INTUITION

Over the years, I have heard a lot of people speak of "women's intuition." Some people have a lot of confidence in it because they argue that it is comparable to a sixth sense that a woman has and similar to a depth of wisdom that men possess. Others seek to declare it a myth, arguing that it is only a way to say that women overthink and pick things apart and that women do it in such detail that they end up forming their own opinions based on what they think the truth is and more often than not they are wrong. I do not offer these comments to set up any struggle, but I have heard a lot of married men confessing that if they had accepted their wives' intuition, they would have been better off. On the other hand, I have seen many women displaying so much arrogance based on their claim that they have this unique "intuition," that I have wondered whether too much credence is given to intuition.

Now, while I have no interest in participating in the debate about "woman's intuition", I do find it of interest, because social scientists have stated that what is called "women's intuition" has to do with women's capacity for reading facial expressions, their motherly disposition for empathy and caring, their great openness for emotional messages, and their deep understanding of relationships. When women forget these unique gifts and participate in the feminist discussion in a way that makes it seem they want to be men, then they lose what might be called the positive view of "intuition."

I do not know how you might think about the intuition of the character named Zipporah, who saved her husband Moses' life, at a time when he could have been killed. But it is my opinion, like that of many commentators that she was profoundly intuitive. Here is what we read in Exodus:

> And it came to pass on the way, at the encampment, that the Lord met him and sought to kill him. Then Zipporah took a sharp stone and cut off the foreskin of her son and cast *it* at *Moses'* feet, and said, "Surely you *are* a husband of blood to me!" So He let him go. Then she said, "*You are* a husband of blood!"—because of the circumcision. - Exodus 4:24-26

The backdrop to the story is that when Moses ran away from the wrath of the Pharaoh in Egypt, he went into the Midian desert, where he met Zipporah. Zipporah was one of the seven daughters of Jethro, otherwise called Reuel and Raguel (cf. Exodus 2:18; 4:24, 25; 18:1-6; Numbers 10:29). The sisters would go to the well to water their father's sheep, but the sheepherders by the well were very unkind to them. They allowed them to wait until they had taken care of their own or their master's sheep before they allowed the sister to water their father's sheep.

One day Moses, while running away from Pharoah, happened by the well. He saw the mistreatment by the sheepherders, and he offered his assistance to the sisters in getting water for their sheep. When the sisters arrived home earlier than usual, they told their father how an Egyptian had helped them. The father sent to invite the Egyptian, who was Moses, to his house. After Moses introduced himself, Jethro was satisfied and asked Moses to live with the family. Soon, Moses and Zipporah fell in love, got married, and had a child. A second son came, and soon after, Moses thought of his people back in Egypt. He saw a vision of God, which impressed him to return to Egypt to help his people. Moses took Zipporah and their two sons and started on their way towards Egypt. As they traveled on, Moses had a most powerful encounter with God. The encounter was a confrontation in which God seemed about to take Moses' life because he failed to carry out the covenant of circumcision. In taking note of the encounter and the possible loss of Moses' life, Zipporah quickly cut off the foreskin of Eliezer and threw it before Moses, calling Moses, "a husband of blood," to her.

Commentators argue that to keep the peace, Moses had evidently ignored his faith tradition of circumcision to please his unbelieving wife. He did not perform the ritual of circumcision -the sign of God's covenant- on his son Eliezer. Therefore, the Lord intervened, as a sign of his displeasure, and struck Moses with a fatal disease. At the severity of the reaction, both Zipporah and Moses became conscience-stricken, and Zipporah yielded. Taking a flint stone, Zipporah severed the boy's foreskin and threw it down at Moses' feet.

One might not know how much intuition was involved, but one can be sure of the moment of inspiration and revelation, for it is clear that not only Moses but Zipporah came to understand God's call in a new way. They sensed what it meant to obey. In fact, I vouch that it was more than intuition, for it takes true inspiration and revelation to understand the significance of the divine commandment. True revelation is given by the Spirit of God. It is like Jesus said to his disciple Peter, on the occasion of the confession at Caesarea Philippi, "Blessed are you, Simon Bar-Jonah, for flesh and blood has not revealed *this* to you, but My Father who is in heaven." (Matthew 16:17). Or like the apostle Paul said to the Corinthians "In the same way no one knows the thoughts of God except the Spirit of God. 12 What we have received is not the spirit of the world, but the Spirit who is from God, so that we may understand what God has freely given us." (1 Corinthians 2:11-12 NIV).

We might extol the value of intuition. Still, we must be careful how much credence we give to it because sometimes, in the honor we give to intuition or scientific thinking and human logic, we fail to appreciate the wisdom of the divine.

In fact, whatever lessons Zipporah learned from the encounter, it must have served her well. Even though she turned back from accompanying Moses on the journey to Egypt, on his return, when he led the children of Israel out of Egypt, and he took Zipporah and their sons from her father's house, Zipporah became his confidant and advisor. Some persons have suggested that Aaron and Miriam were jealous of her because she was chief advisor, and because of the color of her skin, being an Ethiopian. No one needs to be dogmatic here, except to say that Zipporah was faithful in standing beside Moses as the leader. She did not allow the voice of distractors to break her relationship with Moses. She used her wisdom to guide and likely sought the wisdom of her father, Jethro. His insights proved invaluable to Moses as he tried to effectively organize the camp of Israel.

Zipporah, that was her name, meaning "a bird," "a sparrow," the daughter of priest Jethro of Midian, and the wife of Moses, intuitive, inspirational, wise, courageous, faithful, dependable, and truly powerful.

Reflecting on the discussion

1. What new insights that you have gained from the discussion?

2. Has there been an experience that you faced lately that might have turned into defeat, but, by the grace of God, has turned into a triumph?

3. Write a blessing that you desire for today, and for which you need to pray.

DEALING WITH TABOOS

'If a woman has a discharge, *and* the discharge from her body is blood, she shall be [a]set apart seven days; and whoever touches her shall be unclean until evening. [20] Everything that she lies on during her impurity shall be unclean; also, everything that she sits on shall be unclean. [21] Whoever touches her bed shall wash his clothes and bathe in water, and be unclean until evening. [22] And whoever touches anything that she sat on shall wash his clothes and bathe in water, and be unclean until evening. [23] If *anything* is on *her* bed or on anything on which she sits, when he touches it, he shall be unclean until evening. [24] And if any man lies with her at all, so that her impurity is on him, he shall be [b]unclean seven days; and every bed on which he lies shall be unclean.

- **Leviticus 15:19-24 NKJV**

DEALING WITH TABOOS

If you have ever felt like you were mistreated, cheated, and disrespected as a woman, in the contemporary world, try for a moment to keep your pressure down. Take a little time to reflect on the conditions that many women had to face in by-gone days. Notice the differences between by-gone days and today. I am not encouraging you to feel mollified or to accept any abnormal condition of oppression and abuse, but it is always good to take a moment to praise God for changes that have taken place from the old requirements. After your moment of praise, you need to get back to work by making sure that "history does not repeat itself" and that present oppressive conditions are not accepted as the norm. You are not called to take mistreatment and oppression, except for the sake of the preaching of the gospel.

Have you ever thought what it would mean today if women were asked to live under a ceremonial system such as is found in the priestly record of the biblical book of Leviticus? Leviticus is one of the most fascinating books in the Bible that deals with women's issues. Both the priests and people of Israel were given instructions on how the sanctuary worship services should be carried out. Additionally, there were instructions on other topics such as:

1. The rules for birth – What was expected of women when they had a boy child or a girl child. My spouse gets quite upset when

she is reading the book of Leviticus and sees what she thinks is prejudicial treatment in such matters (cf. Leviticus 12-20).

2. Rules for the menstrual cycle – The taboos were so grave that the women were fearful. They were often treated as if they had leprosy. (cf. Leviticus 15:19-33)

3. The rules for unlawful sexual relations – The scales seem tipped in favor of men over against women. Women were punished severely for the same violations as men, yet men were lightly punished, if ever. (Leviticus 18:1-30)

4. The rules of redemption for women, as noted in Leviticus 27, is most intriguing. Here is a list that shows the disparities:

Males 60 and over: 15 shekels
Females 60 and over: 10 shekels
Males ages 20–60: 50 shekels
Females ages 20–60: 30 shekels
Males ages 5–20: 20 shekels
Females ages 5–20: 10 shekels
Males ages 0–5: 5 shekels
Females ages 0–5: 3 shekels

The ceremonial and civil laws in Leviticus demonstrate vast differences in how women were treated over against their male counterparts. But, until one understands the general cultural context in which Leviticus was written, one will feel that Leviticus endorses a low value of women while giving men high worth.

Another way of seeing this is to say that the practical concerns of Leviticus were about cleanliness, purity, and holiness. In fact, how embarrassing it would be, for women, if they appeared in public in an unsanitary condition? Women understood that to stay out of public view for a stated time, was the right thing to do to safeguard their dignity and respect. Within our contemporary frame, in general, there are no such restrictions because of technological advancements. The point of difference is that the Levitical laws were seeking to protect women against those things that would have embarrassed them. One should not trivialize this point.

Today when some individuals or church institutions abuse and oppress women and use Leviticus to support their actions, they need to take note as to what Leviticus was seeking to do, and what Jesus did when he carried forward his mission. For example, Jesus regarded the intrinsic value of women in the ways in how he spoke to them and addressed them (Luke 13). When some of them were having heavy blood flow, Jesus touched them and also allowed them to touch him (cf Luke 13:16). Look at Jesus' response to the woman taken in adultery. While the men wanted to stone her, Jesus did what he did to forgive and free her. (cf. John 4:16-18). He allowed an adulterous woman to wash his feet (Luke 7:44-50). On the morning of his resurrection, Jesus gave the first resurrection message to the three women - Mary Magdalene, Mary, the mother of James, and Salome- who had gone to visit the tomb with spices for his body. To the women, Jesus said, "Go tell my disciples and Peter that I am going ahead of them into Galilee as I have promised." (look at the detail of the resurrection story in Mark 16:1-80). The point being made is that in his ministry, Jesus did all he could to remove many of the restrictions of the Levitical system.

The apostle Paul followed the transformative actions of Jesus by saying to the Galatian Christian church, "There is neither Jew nor Gentile, neither slave nor free, **nor is there male and female**, for you are all one in Christ Jesus." (Galatians 3:28 NIV, emphasis mine).

The point is that while Leviticus might seem biased in the ways that men versus women were treated, it was never intended to be a document of abuse and oppression. Neither was the intent for it to be used in contemporary times to put women down. In fact, when truly understood, Leviticus is a book of liberation, even for women.

A vital lesson to learn is that religion can be trapped in cultural modes that become oppressive instead of liberating. Thus, we should always be careful not to allow the cultural patterns or ceremonial systems of the past to hold us hostage. We should work for the liberty that is offered to all of us in Christ Jesus, our Lord.

Reflecting on the discussion

1. What new insights that you have gained from the discussion?

2. Has there been an experience that you faced lately that might have turned into defeat, but, by the grace of God, has turned into a triumph?

3. Write a blessing that you desire for today, and for which you need to pray.

ARTISTIC WOMEN

All the women who were gifted artisans spun yarn with their hands, and brought what they had spun, of blue, purple, and scarlet, and fine linen. And all the women whose heart stirred with wisdom spun yarn of goats' hair.

– **Exodus 35:25, 26 NKJV**

ARTISTIC WOMEN

When I heard it, once more, that the majority of people across the United States are still not ready to vote for a woman to be president, and also noted that women are not being ordained in some churches to pastoral ministry, I struggled with "why?" Is it because of news media chatter and false prophetic prediction or prejudice or what? I know that some individuals use historical, psychological, economical, traditional, and theological rationalizations to justify their decisions. It seems that none of the areas cited offer up definitive evidence for the conclusions or kind of constraints that are articulated.

Whenever I hear these arguments, because I know that people often speak in religious tones, I run back to my Bible to look at what it says about affirmation and liberation, and how to deal with oppression and persecution. What I have found is that even in what we would call the patriarchal age, often when men were called to lead, women were very much at their sides.

One classic example is the building and furnishing of the ancient sanctuary, as Israel journeyed from Egypt to Canaan, where women worked alongside men. The names most often heard in any recital of the construction and furnishing of the sanctuary are Bezaleel (Exodus 35:30), from the tribe of Judah, and Aholiab (Exodus 35:30,) from the tribe of Dan. We are told how they were gifted in craftsmanship and workmanship and how God placed his Spirit upon them and gave them teaching abilities so that they could help others develop their artesian skills. (cf Exodus 35:31-32). However, the following should be noted carefully:

> All the women *who were* gifted artisans spun yarn with their hands, and brought what they had spun, of blue, purple, *and* scarlet, and fine linen. And all the women whose hearts stirred with wisdom spun yarn of goats' *hair (Exodus 35:25, 26 NKJV).*

Yes, the women were right there, using their skills for the building and decoration of the sanctuary. Just as God filled the men with his Spirit, the women were filled with the Spirit also. And the Spirit stimulated their gifts so that they were equal participants in the work of the sanctuary building and decoration. I do not know that anything better could be said about those women than that they were "wise" and "gifted." I can also think of them working in the background and in the foreground, as is the case in my pastoral ministry. I have seen women work with a fervor and a sincere spirit of self-sacrifice. I have noted in them a genuine sense of commitment that has challenged the men around them. I appreciate their loyalty as they work in the most supportive relationship tirelessly. I appreciate the cooking workshops they conduct, and the weekend sewing classes they lead, trying to teach a younger generation how to sew, knit, crochet, how to be good mothers and professionals, and so on. I have seen them working in the community services and food pantry ministries, lifting boxes, and doing what we have heard that women are "not supposed to do." I have seen them in their prayer warrior support groups. I have seen them, and I am convinced that their contribution to their churches is hardly ever truly appreciated.

And while I do not want to dismiss the excellent work of many women, I have seen a catalog of women's actions that one might call negative. But when I look beyond the negative and mythological presentations that women cannot do this or that, I find that the roles that many filled in history in building families, communities, organizations, and institutions, have been much more significant than is recorded in historical sources.

In the religious sphere, as I have noted, the story of Israel would not be what it has been without the contribution of the women that I have called resisters and rescuers, and in my present reference, in construction of the sanctuary that Moses was commanded to build (cf. Exodus 35). The use of their gifts, their sacrificial offerings, their willingness, their commitment, their passion, their caring, and their worshipful life, made all the difference. They were Spirit-filled and passionate about their work. And they were not afraid to use their hands to carry on the job.

Just like every man is not called to be a leader, so it is that every woman is not called to be a leader, but God has called women like men to help build up "sanctuaries" in varied places of the earth where his kingdom is to be built up. When we think of the contribution in the more extensive work of the Christian church today, we think of the many women who have helped in pioneering missionary work. We also think of how women used their initiative in the rise of the Sunday School Movement in Gloucester, England (1780). Although the initiative for the Movement has been credited to Robert Raikes and Thomas Stock who started it to teach the poor how to read, history would be incomplete if one did not mention Hannah More, who held her first Sunday school in her home in Blagdon, England in 1795. She became very influential to the Sunday school movement with the establishment of her Cheap Repository Tracts. The simple point of observation is that the growth of the Sunday school movement was not left up to men. There are numerous stories told in the United States when many women could not preach from their church's pulpits. Women, it is said, took the sermonic themes and held discussion groups in the basement of their churches or in their homes. Thus, the Sunday/Sabbath school movement, or what is called in my church the Sabbath School, grew out of these initiatives led by women.

Of course, what is being promoted in the above is not how struggle led to the rise of women, but how mutual respect for women's gifts can help to build up the church and the kingdom at large. Whoever has a gift that can be used for the development of God's work needs to use it. The gifts that women possess are to be used in whatever position they can be best used. In this way, the church will be built up, and the kingdom of God will expand. When men and women work cooperatively for the accomplishment of the work, it will be effectively completed.

Reflecting on the discussion

1. What new insights that you have gained from the discussion?

2. Has there been an experience that you faced lately that might have turned into defeat, but, by the grace of God, has turned into a triumph?

3. Write a blessing that you desire for today, and for which you need to pray.

SOCIAL ACTIVISTS

The daughters of Zelophehad ... came forward. The names of the daughters were Mahlah, Noa, Hoglah, Milcah, and Tirzah. They stood before Moses, Eleazar the priest, the chieftains, and the whole assembly, at the entrance of the Tent of Meeting. (27:1-2). Let not our father's name be lost to his clan just because he had no son! Give us a holding among our father's kinsmen!"

– **Numbers 27:3, 4**

SOCIAL ACTIVISTS

As the 400 years history of African slavery is being appraised, even as I write this reflection, we need to be appreciative of the intersection between such history and women who are standing up for their freedom today. It would be fascinating to name some of the freedom fighting women, but the list would be too extensive for this reflection. However, we take note that women should be celebrated as the foundation on which the contemporary generation of courageous women is building their struggle for liberation. In the time of slavery, women had to find their own ways of resistance and rebellion, and women today will need to find their own way. Women should not sit back and wait for men to speak up for them; they are encouraged to speak out for themselves.

One precedent that has excited me is what I read in my Bible about how effective the five daughters of Zelophehad were when they spoke up in their struggle for liberation. Remember them? They were five sisters - Mahlah, Noa, Hoglah, Milcah, and Tirzah - who lived at the end of the Israelites' Exodus from Egypt. As these women prepared to enter the Promised Land, they confronted Joshua and the elders of Israel. They brought their case concerning their right of inheritance to their father's land to the community.

Toward the end of the 40 years of wilderness travel, a census was taken of all males over the age of 20 (v. 2). In the census, it was noted that "Zelophehad had no sons, only daughters" (v. 33). And, as the census concluded, Moses how the land should be apportioned and shared among the males (v, 53). However, the daughters of Zelophehad were not scheduled to receive any property as an inheritance.

These five sisters were expected to accept their fate and keep silent. They were supposed to live according to the social expectation of "women must remain silent in public," but they did not. As the scriptural record states:

> The daughters of Zelophehad ... came forward. The names of the daughters were Mahlah, Noa, Hoglah, Milcah, and Tirzah. They stood before Moses, Eleazar the priest, the chieftains, and the whole assembly, at the entrance of the Tent of Meeting. (27:1-2). Let not our father's name be lost to his clan just because he had no son! Give us a holding among our father's kinsmen!" – Numbers 27:3, 4

After listening to the women's requests, Moses' reaction was apparent. He "brought their case before God" (27:5), listened to God's direction, and then disclosed how God told him to support their demand (27:6-8). The settlement of their claim led to changes in the law of inheritance. Women could now inherit land and pass it on to future generations. These sisters were courageous. They did not spend their time complaining and building up any resentful feelings; they took their case in hand and went to argue it before Moses and the elders. They knew their God-given rights and were not afraid to ask about them.

These sisters had very clear perceptions of what they needed to do. They studied history. They knew the law. They understood the social structure, and they knew how to challenge those aspects of history - the law and the social fabric that were unjust toward them. Many individuals would wish to question history, the law, or the social structure, but that would be a mistake. Such an attitude would be characterized as ignorance and or being too lazy to educate themselves about their history, law, or social structure of their community. As such, they would handicap their ability to effect any real change. This observation might seem harsh, as it is stated, but it is the case today in many places. Ignorance blinds the perception of many, and therefore, there is more anxiety and complaining rather than participating in change. Currently, what we see is a lot of rage and frustration to bring about change.

The latter comment leads me to say that the daughters of Zelophehad must be commended for their extraordinary resolve and determination. They were not rude or crude. They knew how to press their case without "getting into the gutter." When many see the hand of abuse, oppression, and disenfranchisement, they fall into the temptation to use vulgarity and vile behaviors to settle matters. But the example of Zelophehad's daughter is ours.

As Christians, we need to point more to the perfect example of Jesus, who was our world's most celebrated social activist, but who was always "wise as a serpent, and harmless as a dove." He challenged the leaders and the social structures of his time in how he dealt with women, but Jesus was never disrespectful or crude. He worked for the liberation of humanity and has left us the best example on earth.

In effect, while this reflection is intended to encourage social activism, by watching the daughters of Zelophehad, and Jesus, it is never designed to promote anything other than love, justice, and humility. When women are being abused and disenfranchised, no one should think they are to keep silent. When people are being oppressed because of their race or ethnicity, there must be voices to cry out. When there is a need to call for equal pay or any other requirement that will facilitate respect for each other, we must speak up. Just as the daughters of Zelophehad did not sit down in silence, women (and men) are called to stand up, speak up, and change whatever situation needs to be changed by the grace of God.

Reflecting on the discussion

1. What new insights that you have gained from the discussion?

2. Has there been an experience that you faced lately that might have turned into defeat, but, by the grace of God, has turned into a triumph?

3. Write a blessing that you desire for today, and for which you need to pray.

BOUNCING BACK

You shall not pervert the justice due to the stranger or the fatherless, nor take a widow's garment as a pledge. [18] But you shall remember that you were a slave in Egypt, and the Lord your God redeemed you from there; therefore, I command you to do this thing. [19] "When you reap your harvest in your field and forget a sheaf in the field, you shall not go back to get it; it shall be for the stranger, the fatherless, and the widow, that the Lord your God may bless you in all the work of your hands. [20] When you beat your olive trees, you shall not go over the boughs again; it shall be for the stranger, the fatherless, and the widow. [21] When you gather the grapes of your vineyard, you shall not glean *it* afterward; it shall be for the stranger, the fatherless, and the widow.

– **Deuteronomy 24:18-21 NKJV**

BOUNCING BACK

The struggle for justice is extremely loud today. There are calls for environmental justice, economic justice, social justice, restorative justice, racial justice, feminine justice, and justice in other aspects of our world systems. The cry for justice in the public political realm today was a high priority among the biblical prophets from Moses to John of the Revelation. I have chosen to use only a sample from the writings of Moses to demonstrate that matters of justice were a high priority in Bible times. The greatest indictment in the words of the prophets came on the people of God when they failed to practice justice. While you might think that the various forms of justice are disconnected, on careful attention, you will find that they all intersect. And the intersection becomes more evident as one focuses on the family and feminine justice. Thus, my focus in this reflection is primarily on female justice.

Throughout history, women have faced all kinds of life situations that have been unjust. And it is sometimes difficult to see how God works through such conditions for the benefit of women. The book of Deuteronomy provides a basic lesson in how a community in the ancient world struggled to create a system of justice amidst injustice, to enhance the cause of women. Let us look at a few scenarios that have often challenged commentators.

1. In the practice of warfare, the soldiers took women as captives. In the book of Deuteronomy, the soldiers were prohibited from

raping them; they were to be treated with respect. If a soldier (only men were enlisted in those days) chose one of his female prisoners to be his wife, he had to give her time to mourn for her parents, who were evidently killed in the war. After the elapse of time, then he had to marry her. And, in the eventuality, he wanted to put her away, he could not treat her as a slave. He had to allow her to go free (Deuteronomy 21:10-14).

2. When a man married a wife and consummated the marriage, he was not allowed to throw her out or divorce her, as easily as some wished to do. He could not make unsubstantiated claims that she had lost her virginity before the wedding. His wife was to receive his respect. His job was to protect her, rather than to use and abuse her. He was not allowed to bring false charges against her without providing evidence to the court at the city gate. His marriage was for keeps (Deuteronomy 22:13-19). Of course, if his charges of infidelity were correct, then she was stoned to death. (Deuteronomy 22:20-21).

3. If a man had a sexual relationship with a married woman, both of them should die. (Deuteronomy 22:22). The man did not have an easy out.

4. If a man was caught having consensual intercourse with a young woman who was engaged, both had to be put to death (Deuteronomy 22:23). Again, the man did not escape without judgment. If the woman was forced into the activity, and tried to get

away but could not, then she was set free while the man was to be punished (Deuteronomy 22:24).

5. If a man raped a virgin, he would have to pay restitution price of fifty shekels to her father and marry her, because he "humiliated her." (Deuteronomy 22:25).

6. A man should not have intercourse with his father's wife. (Deuteronomy 22:26).

Yes, it is true, if one were writing laws today for the liberation of women around the world, such a one would know that if one wishes to honor the divine, one would have to be written fairly. My point is that the laws in Deuteronomy were already affirming that women should be treated with dignity and justly. Even though there were limitations on what could be done in a culture where women were being treated as the property of their fathers and husbands, efforts were made in the Deuteronomic code to raise the status of women. These efforts were also evident throughout the other writings of Moses.

If we compare what is happening to women in places where the Bible is taken seriously, with what is happening to women, in other world cultures and religions, where the Bible is not given preeminence, we will have to say, "thank God that we have the Bible to teach us about liberation justice for women". Anyone who is using Deuteronomy, or any other part of the Bible to justify the oppression of women, have misunderstood the Bible as a book of liberation. Or we might say, as many commentators have, that throughout the Bible, there is a definite focus on, the poor, slaves, orphans, **widows** and other destitute persons. We might also note that there is judgment threatened against anyone who seeks to hurt such individuals.

The crucial point I wish to make is that while so much has been done in history to put women down, there is a lot to learn. If we would read history through the correct Scriptural lens, we will find enough to help us work for the liberation of women according to the divine design.

Reflecting on the discussion

1. What new insights that you have gained from the discussion?

2. Has there been an experience that you faced lately that might have turned into defeat, but, by the grace of God, has turned into a triumph?

3. Write a blessing that you desire for today, and for which you need to pray.

CONCLUSION

My review of the women of Genesis through Deuteronomy has been a profound blessing to me. It has given me new insights into the lives of the women of that time that were well known to me, and also brought into prominence, obscure women. Several truths became more forceful to me. Here are ten of them:

1. That God cares about women as well as he does men. The gender biases we maintain were never intended by God. From the beginning, he made humanity to be loving, respectful, kind, and courteous to one another. "Male and female he created them."

2. That we are not just born into a curse (Psalm 51:5), but when first created, God put a legacy of blessings on us. And such blessings are still available to all who come into the world – male and female alike.

3. That God will find the most insignificant woman and make her a blessing to the world.

4. That the providence of God works behind all human situations, and though at times, God might seem to be absent from our frame, yet God is always watching as he watched overHagar.

5. That God is not bound to culture as we are – God can pass beyond our social constrictions to work out his purposes for our salvation.

6. That God is not puzzled by our mixed-up situations. He knows our frames and can work through them.

7. That even in a patriarchal age, there were also powerful matriarchs – women who transmitted a powerful influence to future generations.

8. That when people try to help out God, they cause confusion and bring hurt to themselves and the world about them.

9. That resentment is profoundly dangerous when it develops. It leads to rage and outrage, and violent actions that might even surprise its host.

10. That while we might have placed ourselves in the messiest of situations, God always has a way to take us out.

11. That when we are hurting and cry out to God, God listens and intervenes.

12. That through the stories of some of the most imperfect women, the story of salvation is written.

Yes, the reflection on the lives of the women of the Pentateuch has been spell-binding, for me. I cherish the lessons and wish that they might reach the hearts of many who are in similar situations.

www.ingramcontent.com/pod-product-compliance
Lightning Source LLC
LaVergne TN
LVHW041540070426
835507LV00011B/847